Adventures in Reading

BEGINNING

Henry & Melissa Billings
Christy M. Newman

 McGraw Hill Contemporary

 **Contemporary**

Published by McGraw-Hill/Contemporary, a business unit of The McGraw-Hill Companies, Inc., 1221 Avenue of the Americas, New York, NY 10020. Copyright © 2002, 1996, 1990, 1985 by The McGraw-Hill Companies, Inc. All rights reserved. No part of this publication may be reproduced or distributed in any form or by any means, or stored in a database or retrieval system, without the prior written consent of The McGraw-Hill Companies, Inc., including, but not limited to, in any network or other electronic storage or transmission, or broadcast for distance learning.

Some ancillaries, including electronic and print components, may not be available to customers outside the United States.

 This book is printed on recycled, acid-free paper containing 10% postconsumer waste.

1 2 3 4 5 6 7 8 9 0 QPD/QPD 0 9 8 7 6 5 4 3 2

ISBN: 0-07-254601-8
ISBN: 0-07-121370-8 (ISE)

Editorial director: *Tina B. Carver*
Senior managing editor: *Erik Gundersen*
Developmental editor: *Linda O'Roke*
Director of North American marketing: *Thomas P. Dare*
Director of international marketing and sales: *Kate Oakes*
Production manager: *Genevieve Kelley*
Cover designer: *Michael Kelly*
Interior designer: *Don Kye, Think Design LLC*
Art: *Anthony Lewis*
Copyeditor: *Sophia Wisener*
Skills indexer: *Talbot Hamlin*
Proofreader: *Becky Keys*

INTERNATIONAL EDITION ISBN: 0-07-121370-8

www.mhcontemporary.com

The **McGraw·Hill** Companies

Acknowledgements

The publisher would like to thank the following educational professionals whose comments, reviews, and assistance were instrumental in the development of *Adventures in Reading*.

Carolyn Bohlman, *Main East High School (Chicago, IL)*
Suzanne Gut, *Palm Beach Community College (FL)*
Greg Keech, *City College of San Francisco*
Elizabeth Minicz, *William Rainey Harper College (Chicago, IL)*
Paula Orias, *Broward County Public Schools (FL)*
Sally Peckenham, *Mt. Diablo Unified School District (CA)*
Stephen Sloan, *Los Angeles Unified School District*
Arlene Simmons, *Los Angeles Unified School District*
Leslie Eloise Somers, *Miami-Dade County Public Schools*
David Thormann, *City College of San Francisco*
Joanne H. Urrutia, *Miami-Dade County Public Schools*
Travis Venters, *Obirin University, Japan*

The authors would like to thank the following McGraw-Hill/Contemporary staff members for their support and assistance in the development of *Adventures in Reading*.

Louis Carrillo, Tina Carver, Amy Chen, Tom Dare, Paula Eacott, Erik Gundersen, Thomas Healy, Kristina Hue, Nancy Jordan, Genevieve Kelley, Mike Kelly, Kareen Kjelstrup, Maxine McCormick, Kate Oakes, Spike Lim, Sam Lin, Yoshio Kimura, Hajime Shishido, and Anne Petti Smith.

Thanks to Linda O'Roke for her guidance and support — Melissa and Henry Billings

Thanks to Jonathan, Corey, and Tom for everything — Christy Newman

Introduction

Adventures in Reading is a three-book series for students of English as a second or foreign language that includes the following titles:

- *Adventures in Reading—Beginning*
- *Adventures in Reading—High Beginning*
- *Adventures in Reading—Intermediate*

Each book contains 16 six-page chapters that develop reading comprehension and vocabulary building skills around high-interest reading passages. Adventure-based reading passages profile exciting pursuits like biking down a volcano, running a marathon, and discovering an underground city.

All of the stories in *Adventures in Reading—Beginning* are 250–350 words in length. Passages in the High Beginning book run 350–400 words in length, and at the Intermediate level the reading selections are 400–500 words long. The reading and vocabulary skill building activities throughout the book prepare students for success on a variety of standardized tests. The array of reading and vocabulary building skills covered in this book is outlined in the Scope & Sequence. Also, the Skills Index at the back of this book shows teachers where each skill is introduced and recycled.

Components

The complete *Adventures in Reading—Beginning* program includes the following components:

- Student book
- Teacher's manual featuring:
    - -- answer key
    - -- chapter quizzes
    - -- vocabulary cloze activities for each chapter
- Audio cassette/CD with recordings of all reading passages

Guide to Adventures in Reading

CHAPTER 7

Biking Down a Volcano

1. fishing   2. lake   3. forest   4. mountain biking   5. beach

Key Vocabulary

Complete the sentences with a word from the picture.

a. When you try to catch a fish, you are _____

b. You can go fishing at the ocean or on a _____.

c. When you ride a bicycle up and down big hills, you are _____

d. Many trees in one area are called a _____

e. The _____ is where the ocean and the land meet.

Before You Read

Read the chapter title and look at the picture. What does th___
Read the story to check your guess.

Ⓐ Go mountain biking   Ⓑ Go fishing   Ⓒ Go swim___

Chapter-opening art visually introduces students to the theme of the reading. This art also provides a context for the words introduced in **Key Vocabulary**.

In **Key Vocabulary**, students match new words to the pictures above. This *picture dictionary approach* to vocabulary building prepares students to tackle the reading more successfully.

Before You Read questions ask students to make predictions about the reading. Students then read the passage to check their predictions.

Comprehension will increase for many students as they listen to an *audio recording* of the reading.

Key Vocabulary items introduced at the beginning of the chapter appear in bold-faced type in the reading.

The *globe* icon leads students to maps at the back of the book to locate places in the reading.

Every fifth line in the reading passage is numbered for easy reference.

Biking Down a Volcano

Every year Valerie and Richard Benson go on a nice vacation. Sometimes they go to the **beach**. Sometimes they go to the mountains. Valerie's favorite sport is **fishing**, so sometimes Valerie and Richard go to a **lake** and fish.

5   This year Richard wants to do something new. He loves riding his bike. He wants to go **mountain biking**. Valerie doesn't like biking. She really doesn't like riding up hills.

"I'll make a deal with you," she tells Richard. "We can go mountain biking, but I choose the place."

10   Richard says OK. He doesn't care about the place. He just wants to go mountain biking.

Valerie turns on her computer and logs on to the Internet. She uses a search engine and types in two words: biking and Hawaii.

Soon Valerie finds a good Web site. It is for a biking company on 15   Maui, a Hawaiian island. This company has the perfect bike trip for Valerie. She sends an e-mail to get more information.

"We are going mountain biking in Hawaii," Valerie tells Richard at dinner. Richard is happy. He thinks about biking on the coast and in the **forest**.

20   In Hawaii he learns the truth. Richard and Valerie are going

See Page 117

mountain biking, but it is all downhill! The biking company drives them to the top of a volcano called Haleakala. Then Valerie and Richard bike 38 miles down to the ocean. Both Richard and Valerie enjoy their bike ride.

"This is great!" says Richard. "Can we do it again tomorrow?"

Comprehension questions check students' understanding of the reading passages.

Comprehension

True or False? Fill in the correct bubble.   True   False

1. Valerie and Richard always vacation in Hawaii. ...... Ⓣ ...... Ⓕ
2. Richard only likes to bike downhill. .... Ⓣ ...... Ⓕ
3. Valerie finds a good vacation place online. .... Ⓣ ...... Ⓕ
4. Richard wants to bike down Haleakala again. ...... Ⓣ ...... Ⓕ
5. Valerie is good at using the Internet. .... Ⓣ ...... Ⓕ

By working with **standardized testing formats**, students prepare for success on a variety of standardized exams.

Inference questions are marked with a **light bulb** icon. These questions help students read more critically.

Main Idea

What is the main idea of this story? Fill in the correct bubble.

① Valerie and Richard like Hawaii.
② There's a good mountain bike company on Maui.
③ Valerie plans a good mountain bike riding trip.
④ Richard and Valerie don't like the same sports.

Reading Skill: Making Inferences

To **make an inference** you use what is *written* in a story to guess at something that is *not* written. You can understand more about the story when you make inferences.

Information from the story	Inference
Valerie finds a vacation place using the Internet. →	Valerie knows how to use the Internet to find information.

1. Read the conversation.

Richard: Let's ride our bikes to the beach.
Valerie: We can't right now. The bikes are in the car. First, we go to the top of the volcano. Then we ride 38 miles to the bottom.
Richard: Is the whole ride downhill?
Valerie: Yes. It's the only way to go!
Richard: Really? That's great!

2. Underline the best answer. Write it on the line.
    a. Richard and Valerie are __In Hawaii__ (at home, in Hawaii).
    b. They are talking .... (after, before) they ride down the volcano.
    c. Richard is .... (surprised, sad) that the bike ride is all downhill.

Making inferences, identifying cause and effect, and many other **reading skills** are taught and recycled throughout the book.

Vocabulary Review

Complete the sentences. Write the missing word.

beach	forest	fishing	lake	mountain biking

1. Richard and Valerie like .... down the volcano.
2. Richard likes biking and walking in the .... He likes to look at the trees and animals.
3. Valerie and Richard's hotel is on the .... They see the ocean from their room.
4. Valerie is very good at .... She usually catches a lot of fish.
5. Sometimes they go fishing on a ....

In **Vocabulary Review**, students test their understanding of key vocabulary introduced at the beginning of the chapter.

Guide to Adventures in Reading

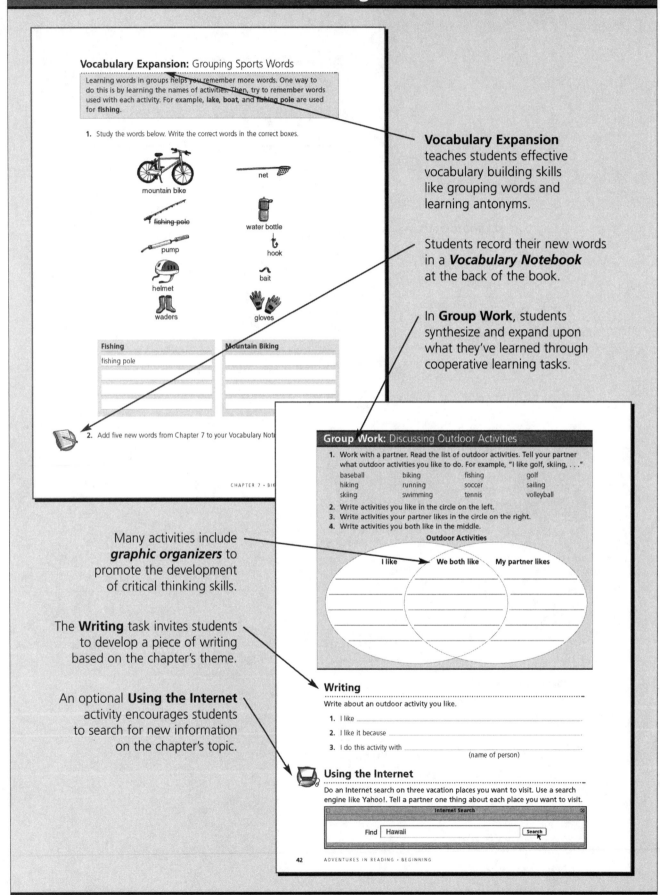

Vocabulary Expansion: Grouping Sports Words

Learning words in groups helps you remember more words. One way to do this is by learning the names of activities. Then, try to remember words used with each activity. For example, **lake**, **boat**, and **fishing pole** are used for **fishing**.

1. Study the words below. Write the correct words in the correct boxes.

mountain bike

net

fishing pole

water bottle

pump

hook

helmet

bait

waders

gloves

Fishing	Mountain Biking
fishing pole	

2. Add five new words from Chapter 7 to your Vocabulary Not...

CHAPTER 7 · BIK...

Vocabulary Expansion teaches students effective vocabulary building skills like grouping words and learning antonyms.

Students record their new words in a **Vocabulary Notebook** at the back of the book.

In **Group Work**, students synthesize and expand upon what they've learned through cooperative learning tasks.

Group Work: Discussing Outdoor Activities

1. Work with a partner. Read the list of outdoor activities. Tell your partner what outdoor activities you like to do. For example, "I like golf, skiing, . . ."

baseball	biking	fishing	golf
hiking	running	soccer	sailing
skiing	swimming	tennis	volleyball

2. Write activities you like in the circle on the left.
3. Write activities your partner likes in the circle on the right.
4. Write activities you both like in the middle.

Outdoor Activities

I like   We both like   My partner likes

Many activities include **graphic organizers** to promote the development of critical thinking skills.

The **Writing** task invites students to develop a piece of writing based on the chapter's theme.

An optional **Using the Internet** activity encourages students to search for new information on the chapter's topic.

Writing

Write about an outdoor activity you like.

1. I like _____
2. I like it because _____
3. I do this activity with _____
   (name of person)

Using the Internet

Do an Internet search on three vacation places you want to visit. Use a search engine like Yahoo!. Tell a partner one thing about each place you want to visit.

Internet Search	⊠
Find Hawaii	Search

42   ADVENTURES IN READING · BEGINNING

viii

Table of Contents

Scope and Sequence

Vocabulary Expansion	Group Work	Internet Search Topics
Grouping Words	Talking about Jobs	New York City
Using Prepositions of Time	Finding Someone Who… Likes Different Sports	Boston Marathon
Learning Sense Words	Interviewing People About Favorite Animals	Favorite Animal
Grouping Food Words	Discussing Food and Drinks	Sandstorms
Learning Neighborhood Words	Talking About Stores	Homeless Shelters
Grouping Words	Asking People About Home Activities	Boy Scouts
Grouping Sports Words	Discussing Outdoor Activities	Vacation Places
Learning Opposite Pairs	Sharing Vacation Stories	Vietnam
Grouping School Words	Talking about Your Classroom	High School Clubs
Grouping Food Words	Planning a Menu	Recipes
Describing the Weather	Talking About Family Activities	Weather
Learning *A* and *A Pair Of*	Choosing Clothes for a Trip	Clothing Stores
Grouping Household Words	Talking About Homes	Renting a Home
Learning Computer Terms	Comparing Free Time Activities	Robot Wrestling
Grouping Words	Interviewing People About Helpful Animals	Dolphins
Grouping Words	Planning a Vacation	Australia

Driving a Taxi in New York

Key Vocabulary

Match the sentences to the items in the picture.

a. **Construction workers** build buildings. ___1___

b. A **taxi driver** drives people around for money. _____

c. **Paramedics** drive sick people to the hospital. _____

d. A **passenger** rides in the taxi. _____

e. A taxi **fare** is the money the passenger pays. _____

Before You Read

Look at the chapter title and the picture. What do you think the story is about? Read the story to check your guess.

Ⓐ A taxi driver's work day   Ⓑ Traffic in New York   Ⓒ Vacation

Driving a Taxi in New York

Ted Harrison's day begins at 6:00 a.m. He opens the door of his taxi, gets in, and turns on the engine. This is the start of his 12-hour shift.

Ted is a **taxi driver** in New York City. It is a hard job. "Some **passengers** are happy and friendly," says Ted. "But others are rude.
5 Many people are in a hurry. A few passengers try to take my money."

Today begins well. Ted's first passenger wants to go to John F. Kennedy International Airport. It's a long ride. The woman pays the **fare.** She gives Ted a big tip.

Then things start to go wrong. Ted gets a flat tire. Next,
10 **construction workers** are working on a new building. Ted waits a long time.

At noon, a woman gets into Ted's taxi. She needs a ride home, so Ted starts to drive. Suddenly, the woman looks sick. Ted stops the taxi. The woman is in a lot of pain. She holds her hand over her heart. The air
15 is cool, but she is hot. Ted thinks she is having a heart attack.

Luckily, Ted knows what to do. He calls 911 on his radio and then he opens a bottle of pills. The pills are aspirins. He gives one to the woman and tells her to eat it. The aspirin thins her blood and helps her stay alive.

20 Soon the ambulance comes. Yes, it is a heart attack. The **paramedics** thank Ted for helping and take the woman to the hospital. Thanks to Ted, the woman is all right.

See Page 117

911= emergency telephone number

Comprehension

True or False? Fill in the correct bubble.

		True	False
1.	Ted drives his taxi 12 hours a day.	T	F
2.	His passengers are always nice.	T	F
3.	A woman gets sick on her way home.	T	F
4.	Ted drives her to the hospital.	T	F
5.	Ted likes to help his passengers.	T	F

Main Idea

What is the main idea of this story? Fill in the correct bubble.

1. All taxi passengers are rude.

2. Ted gets a big tip.

3. Aspirin is good for a heart attack.

4. Ted works hard and helps a passenger.

Reading Skill: Identifying Cause and Effect

Identifying cause and effect helps you see connections.
A **cause** makes something happen. An **effect** is what happens.

Cause
There is a nail on the road.

Effect
Ted's taxi has a flat tire.

Match the **cause** and the **effect**.

Cause

1. Ted is a good taxi driver.
2. Cars, buses, and taxis stop for construction workers.
3. A woman has a heart attack.
4. The woman eats an aspirin.
5. Ted works for 12 hours.

Effect

a. She is in a lot of pain.
b. His passengers give him big tips.
c. The aspirin thins her blood.
d. He is very tired.
e. People are late to work.

Vocabulary Review

Look at the bold words. Fill in the correct bubble.

1. A **taxi driver** gives people _____.
   Ⓐ tips   Ⓑ rides   Ⓒ fares

2. **Passengers** in a taxi do NOT _____.
   Ⓐ pay a fare   Ⓑ drive   Ⓒ tip

3. **Construction workers** make _____.
   Ⓐ buildings   Ⓑ taxis   Ⓒ ambulances

4. **Paramedics** help sick people in _____.
   Ⓐ a taxi   Ⓑ an ambulance   Ⓒ the hospital

5. Another word for **fare** is _____.
   Ⓐ ride   Ⓑ tip   Ⓒ price

Vocabulary Expansion: Grouping Words

Putting new words in groups can help you remember them. For example:

Worker
taxi driver
clerk
teacher
secretary

1. Put the words into the correct groups.

<del>ambulance driver</del>   income   salary

client   money   salesperson

customer   operator   shopper

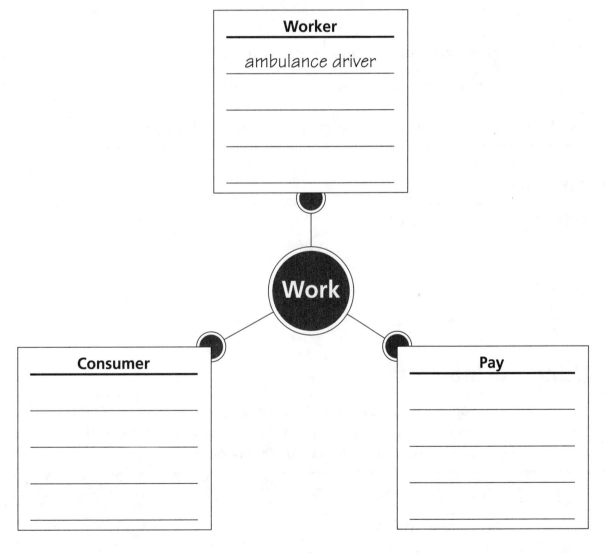

Worker

ambulance driver

Work

Consumer

Pay

2. Add five new words from Chapter 1 to your Vocabulary Notebook on page 97.

Group Work: Talking About Jobs

1. Read the sentences. Fill in **yes** or **no**.

I want to work . . .	Yes	No
in an office.	Y	N
at home.	Y	N
in a store.	Y	N
in a restaurant.	Y	N
with children.	Y	N
alone.	Y	N
part-time.	Y	N
full-time.	Y	N
on weekends.	Y	N

2. Think of two good jobs for you. Write them down.

Two good jobs for me: _____ and _____

3. In small groups, tell your classmates why you like these jobs.

Writing

Write about your favorite city.

1. My favorite city is _____ .

2. I like it because _____ .

3. The best thing about my favorite city is _____ .

 # Using the Internet

Do an Internet search about New York City. Use a search engine like Yahoo!.
Visit two Web sites or more. Tell a partner three things about New York.
For example, New York has more than 8,000,000 people.

Internet Search	☒
Find **New York City**	Search

CHAPTER 2

Running the Boston Marathon

① _____morning_____ 8:00 AM

② _____ 12:00 PM

③ _____ 4:00 PM

④ _____ 7:00 PM

Key Vocabulary
....
Write the words in the correct places above.

    afternoon   **evening**   ~~**morning**~~   **noon**

Before You Read
....
Look at the chapter title and the pictures. Why are the women tied together?
Read the story to check your guess.

Ⓐ They are good friends.

Ⓑ One woman is blind.

Ⓒ They fall down a lot.

Running the Boston Marathon

Kathy Wang runs in the **morning**. She runs early in the **afternoon** and late in the **evening**. Her friends think she's crazy. "Relax," they say. "Slow down."

But Kathy has a goal. She wants to run the Boston Marathon.

See Page 117

5 Thousands of people run this 26.2-mile (42.2 km) race every year. "I know I can't win," Kathy says. "But I want to finish."

Kathy is blind. She can't see. She runs with a partner named Janet Lee. Every day Janet guides Kathy through the streets. Janet ties a string around Kathy's left wrist. She ties the other end around her own

10 right wrist. Kathy feels Janet turn left or right.

On the day of the race, Kathy is excited. At 11:30 a.m., she and Janet go to the starting line. The marathon starts at **noon**. At first the runners are all together. Soon everyone moves apart. Kathy feels strong. She and Janet run mile after mile. At 1:30 p.m. they run past a college.

15 The students cheer and Kathy smiles.

At 2:15 p.m., she is halfway up Heartbreak Hill. Many runners stop on this big hill. Kathy wants to stop. Her legs and her feet hurt. She is not smiling, but she keeps going.

Finally, Kathy is at the top of Heartbreak Hill. There are no more

20 big hills. Kathy is very tired, but she doesn't stop. She crosses the finish line at 3:50 p.m. She hugs Janet. Kathy is now a marathon runner.

Comprehension

Complete the sentences. Fill in the correct bubble.

1. Kathy Wang can't _____.
   (A) see   (B) hear   (C) talk

2. Janet Lee is Kathy's _____.
   (A) mother   (B) running partner   (C) classmate

3. Kathy and Janet's _____ are tied together.
   (A) wrists   (B) legs   (C) fingers

4. Kathy _____ when she is tired.
   (A) quits   (B) keeps running   (C) stops

5. Heartbreak Hill is _____ for runners.
   (A) easy   (B) nice   (C) difficult

Main Idea

What is the main idea of this story? Fill in the correct bubble.

1. Runners' feet hurt.

2. The Boston Marathon is a long race.

3. Kathy works hard and runs a marathon.

4. Janet and Kathy are good friends.

Reading Skill: Finding Details

> **Finding details** gives you information about people and things.
> We ask questions with **who, where,** or **when** to **find details** about a reading.
>
> | **Who?** | → person | (Who is blind?) |
> | **Where?** | → place | (Where is the marathon?) |
> | **When?** | → time | (When does the Boston Marathon start?) |

Find details in the story to answer the questions. Write your answer on the line.

| 3:50 p.m. | Boston | Heartbreak Hill | Janet Lee | ~~Kathy Wang~~ | noon |

1. Who is blind?   <u>Kathy Wang</u>

2. Who is Kathy's running partner? _____

3. Where is the marathon? _____

4. Where do many runners stop running? _____

5. When does the Boston Marathon start? _____

6. When does Kathy cross the finish line? _____

Vocabulary Review

Complete the sentences. Fill in the correct bubble.

1. Kathy is at the starting line at 11:30 in the _____.
   (A) morning   (B) afternoon   (C) evening

2. The race starts 30 minutes later at _____.
   (A) evening   (B) midnight   (C) noon

3. Kathy finishes the race at 3:50 in the _____.
   (A) night   (B) morning   (C) afternoon

4. After the race, Kathy goes to a party at 7:30 in the _____.
   (A) morning   (B) afternoon   (C) evening

Vocabulary Expansion: Using Prepositions of Time

> We use **in** with **a period of time**. For example, we say **in the morning**. We use **at** with **a point in time**. For example, we say **at 11:30 a.m.**

1. Write *in* or *at* on each line.

a.m. (before noon)	p.m. (after noon)
__in__ the morning	_____ the afternoon
_____ 8:15 a.m.	_____ 3:30 p.m.
	_____ 7:45 p.m.
	_____ the evening

2. Now write the times in the box below.

Morning	Afternoon	Evening
in the morning	at 3:30 p.m.	

3. Add five new words from Chapter 2 to your Vocabulary Notebook on page 97.

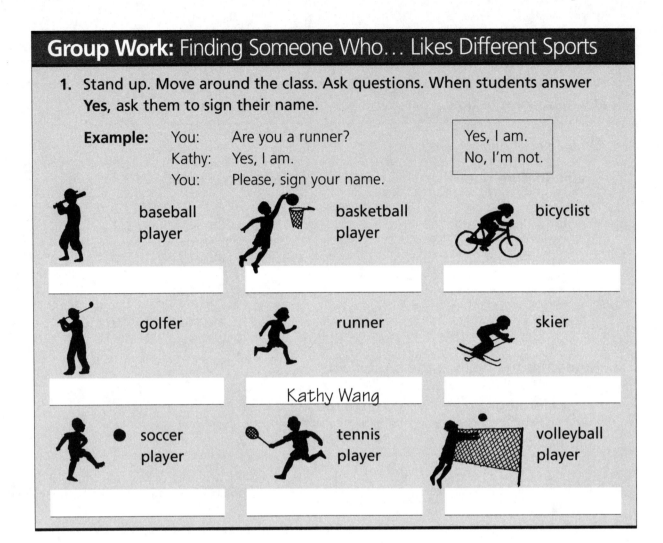

Group Work: Finding Someone Who... Likes Different Sports

1. Stand up. Move around the class. Ask questions. When students answer **Yes**, ask them to sign their name.

   Example:
   You: Are you a runner?
   Kathy: Yes, I am.
   You: Please, sign your name.

   > Yes, I am.
   > No, I'm not.

   baseball player

   basketball player

   bicyclist

   golfer

   runner

   Kathy Wang

   skier

   soccer player

   tennis player

   volleyball player

Writing

Write about a sport you like to watch.

1. I like to watch _____ .

2. My favorite athlete or team is _____ .

3. I like this sport because _____ .

Using the Internet

Do an Internet search about the Boston Marathon. Use a search engine like Yahoo!. Visit two Web sites or more. Tell a partner three things about the Boston Marathon.

Internet Search	☒
Find Boston Marathon	Search

CHAPTER 3

The Search for Bobby

1. police officer   **2. worried**   **3. nose**   **4. sniff**   **5. ground**

Key Vocabulary
....
Complete the sentences with a word from the pictures.

a. The father looks unhappy. He is _____ about his child.

b. The _____ helps the child's parents.

c. Dogs _____ with their noses.

d. The man uses his eyes to see and his _____ to smell.

e. The dog puts its nose on the _____ .

Before You Read
....
Look at the chapter title and the pictures. What is the dog doing? Read the
story to check your guess.

(A) Playing   (B) Looking for someone   (C) Exercising

The Search for Bobby

Alan Stark loves his dog, Molly. He loves her long ears. He loves her brown eyes. But most of all, he loves her **nose**. Molly's nose makes her a special dog.

Molly is a bloodhound. A bloodhound can smell things that
5 other animals can't smell.

See Page 117

The police in Springfield, Ohio, know Molly well. She helps them find missing people. One afternoon a **police officer** calls Alan Stark and says, "It's an emergency."

The officer asks, "Can you and Molly come to 36 Water Street?
10 Bobby Larson is missing. His parents can't find him. They are very **worried**. There is a dangerous river near their house. Can you and Molly help us find Bobby?"

"Yes, we can," says Alan.

It is getting late. It's already cold and dark. Alan and Molly get to
15 work. Alan gets a blanket from Bobby's bedroom. Molly **sniffs** the blanket. It smells like Bobby. It has Bobby's scent.

Then Alan says, "Find!" Molly puts her nose to the **ground**. She finds Bobby's scent and follows it. Alan holds onto the dog and runs behind her. Molly is strong. She pulls Alan from street to street. She
20 pulls him to the river. Finally, Alan sees a boy by the river. It is Bobby.

Bobby is cold, but safe. Bobby's parents are so happy to see him!

They hug him, and they hug Alan. They hug Molly, too.

Now Bobby wants a dog like Molly.

Comprehension

True or False? Fill in the correct bubble.

		True	False
1.	Bobby's nose is very special.	T	F
2.	Molly helps find people.	T	F
3.	Bobby is by the river.	T	F
4.	Alan tells Molly, "Find!"	T	F
5.	Alan probably likes dogs.	T	F

Main Idea

What is the main idea of this story? Fill in the correct bubble.

1. Children sometimes get lost.

2. A dog named Molly finds a lost boy.

3. It's hard to find children at night.

4. Alan Stark has a dog.

Reading Skill: Putting Events in Order

Putting events in order helps you understand the story's action.
To put events in order, look for words like **first**, **second**, **next**, and **last**.

Fill in the sentences with the correct word from the box.

~~First~~	Second	Next	Last

1. _____, Molly sniffs Bobby's blanket.

2. _____, Molly finds Bobby.

3. _____ First _____, the police call Alan for help.

4. _____, Molly gets Bobby's scent.

Vocabulary Review

Complete the sentences. Write the missing word.

ground	nose	police officer	sniffs	worried

1. Molly _____ the blanket to get Bobby's scent.

2. The floor is inside. The _____ is outside.

3. Molly smells with her _____.

4. Bobby is missing. His parents are _____.

5. The _____ helps find Bobby.

Vocabulary Expansion: Learning Sense Words

Learning words that are used together can help you remember them. For example: We **smell** with our **noses**. We **see** with our **eyes**.

Molly's nose has a special sense of smell. People have five senses.

Senses		Body Parts
smell	➤	nose
sight	➤	eyes
hearing	➤	ears
touch	➤	fingers
taste	➤	tongue

1. What do we do with our nose, eyes, ears, fingers, and tongue? Write the correct body part on each line.

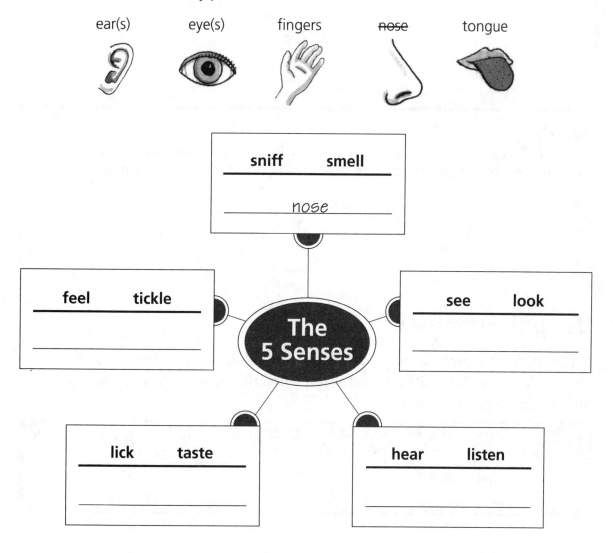

ear(s)   eye(s)   fingers   ~~nose~~   tongue

sniff   smell

_____nose_____

feel   tickle

The 5 Senses

see   look

lick   taste

hear   listen

2. Add five new words from Chapter 3 to your Vocabulary Notebook on page 98.

Group Work: Interviewing People About Favorite Animals

Interview five classmates. Ask them about their favorite animals. Complete the chart.

A: What's your favorite animal?
B: A dog.
A: Why?
B: Dogs are friendly, cute, and nice.

Name	What is your favorite animal?	Why do you like that animal?
Bobby	dog	friendly, cute, nice

Writing

Look around the room. Write one thing that you see, hear, and smell.

1. I see _____ .

2. I hear _____ .

3. I smell _____ .

 ## Using the Internet

Do an Internet search about your favorite animal. Use a search engine like Yahoo!. Visit two Web sites or more. Tell a partner three things you learned about your favorite animal.

Internet Search	⊠
Find dog	Search

CHAPTER 4

Kindness in the Desert

Key Vocabulary

Match the sentences to the items in the picture.

a. The man is **thirsty**. He needs water. ___1___

b. The girl has a bag of **rice**. _____

c. **Dinner** is the evening meal. _____

d. The boy is **hungry**. He wants to eat. _____

e. The woman puts food on the **plate**. _____

Before You Read

Look at the chapter title and the picture. Where do you think the people are?
Read the story to check your guess.

     (A) The Middle East   (B) Europe   (C) South America

Kindness in the Desert

See Page 115

Abdul Mohammed lives in the Syrian Desert. His wife and three

children live with him. Their home is a large tent. There are no other

tents for many miles. Abdul and his family move from place to

place every few months. They look for fresh food for their animals.

5 It is a hard life, but Abdul and his family are happy.

One afternoon Abdul sees a black cloud in the sky. He knows what

it is. A sandstorm is coming. Abdul tells his family to go inside the tent.

Sandstorms are dangerous. Strong wind blows sand everywhere. The

wind and sand sometimes kill people.

10 Abdul starts to go inside. Then he sees a man coming toward him.

Abdul does not know the man. But Abdul quickly invites the stranger

into the tent.

Abdul's wife Salma is not surprised. Abdul always invites strangers

into their home. He and Salma are Bedouin Arabs. In their culture a

15 stranger is always welcome.

This stranger is on his way to visit friends in Saudi Arabia. He is

hot and **thirsty**. He is also scared. The sandstorm is getting closer. The

sky is dark. The wind blows very hard.

Abdul tells the man to relax and gives him a glass of water. Abdul

20 thinks the man is **hungry**. Salma cooks a special **dinner**. She brings out

a **plate** of **rice** and lamb. Abdul and Salma are poor, but they share what they have with the stranger.

Soon the wind stops. The storm is over. The stranger is ready to leave. He thanks Abdul again and again. Abdul smiles. He likes to help
25 strangers. It makes him happy.

Comprehension

Complete the sentences. Fill in the correct bubble.

1. Abdul and his family like living in the _____.
   (A) desert   (B) city   (C) country

2. The family is safe in the _____.
   (A) tent   (B) apartment   (C) house

3. The stranger is going to _____.
   (A) Lebanon   (B) Syria   (C) Saudi Arabia

4. Salma makes rice and lamb for _____.
   (A) breakfast   (B) lunch   (C) dinner

☀ 5. Abdul _____ inviting strangers into his home.
   (A) dislikes   (B) likes   (C) hates

Main Idea

What is the main idea of this story? Fill in the correct bubble.

(1) The desert can be a dangerous place.

(2) A Bedouin mother makes dinner.

(3) A man gets lost in a sandstorm.

(4) A Bedouin family helps a stranger during a sandstorm.

Reading Skill: Making Inferences

Making inferences helps you understand more about a story. To make an inference you use what is *written* in a story to guess at something that is *not written*.

Information from the story
Abdul sees a dark cloud.

Inference
A sandstorm is coming.

Match the **information** and the **inference**.

Information

1. Abdul sees a dark cloud.

2. The family runs into the tent.

3. The stranger is thirsty.

4. Abdul invites the stranger into the tent. Salma isn't surprised.

5. The family needs to find fresh food for the animals.

Inference

a. It is dangerous to be outside.

b. They move from place to place.

c. Abdul often invites strangers into the tent.

d. A sandstorm is coming.

e. He wants a drink of water.

Vocabulary Review

Complete the sentences. Write the missing word.

dinner	hungry	plate	rice	thirsty

1. Salma brings out a _____ of food.

2. The boy is _____. He wants some food.

3. The evening meal is called _____.

4. The family eats _____ for dinner.

5. The man has no water. He is _____.

Vocabulary Expansion: Grouping Food Words

> Grouping words can help you remember them.
> For example, **rice**, **pasta**, and **potatoes** are all **food** words.

1. Look at the pictures.

coffee

bananas

milk

fish

tea

pasta

juice

bread

2. Write the words in the correct boxes.

Drinks	Food
	pasta

3. Circle what you like to eat and drink. Compare your work with a partner.

4. Add five new words from Chapter 4 to your Vocabulary Notebook on page 98.

Group Work: Discussing Food and Drinks

1. Take five minutes.
   Write all of the food words you know.
   Write all of the drink words you know.

Food	Drinks
lamb, rice	water

2. Compare your lists with three classmates. Add three new words to your lists.

Writing

Write about what you want to eat and drink for your next meal.

1. I want to eat _____
   because _____ .

2. I want to drink _____
   because _____ .

 ## Using the Internet

Do an Internet search about sandstorms. Use a search engine like Yahoo!. Visit two Web sites or more. Tell a partner three things you learned about sandstorms.

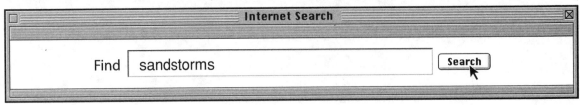

Internet Search

Find | sandstorms | Search

CHAPTER 5

Don't Throw That Food Away

1. supermarket   **2. bakery**   **3. homeless shelter**   **4. bread**   **5. block**

Key Vocabulary

Complete the sentences with a word from the picture.

a. The woman has _____ in her bag. She likes to make sandwiches.

b. The Helping Hands Shelter is a _____. Poor people can go there to eat and sleep.

c. Value More is a _____. People buy food there.

d. People buy bread, cakes, and cookies at a _____.

e. Value More, Fred's Bakery, and Helping Hands Shelter are on the same _____.

Before You Read

Look at the chapter title and the picture. Where is the woman going? Read the story to check your guess.

(A) To the bakery   (B) To the homeless shelter   (C) Home

Don't Throw That Food Away

There are two things Florence Rizzo really hates. First, she hates waste. It upsets her when people throw away good things. Second, she hates it when people have nothing to eat. She thinks no one should be hungry.

5 Florence works hard to stop waste and hunger. Every evening she goes to the **supermarket**. She asks the manager for food he throws away. She takes damaged cans. She takes old boxes of cereal. She gets **bread** that is a little old but good. Florence takes the food to a **homeless shelter** on the same **block**. Workers at the shelter give the food to

10 hungry people.

The supermarket manager gives Florence a lot of food, but it isn't enough. "I need to find more food," says Florence.

So today Florence goes to Fred's **Bakery**. Fred owns the bakery. He sells fresh bread, cakes, and cookies. Every afternoon he throws away

15 bread that he does not sell. Florence thinks this is a big waste. The bread is good.

"Please don't throw away your old bread," she says. "A lot of poor people need it."

"I know it's a waste," says Fred. "But what can I do?"

20 "Give it to me," says Florence. "I can come every day to pick it up. I can take it to the homeless shelter."

> Fred likes this idea. Fred shakes Florence's hand. "Good idea," he says. "Come by the bakery tomorrow at 5:00 p.m. You can pick up some bread."
>
> "Thank you," says Florence. "Together we can help a lot of people."

Comprehension

True or False? Fill in the correct bubble.   **True**   **False**

1. Florence works at a bakery. . . . . T . . . . . . F

2. Florence helps people in her neighborhood. . . . . T . . . . . . F

3. The supermarket manager gives Florence a lot of food. T . . . . . . F

4. Fred gives Florence some rice. . . . . T . . . . . . F

💡 5. Fred wants to help homeless people. . . . . T . . . . . . F

Main Idea

What is the main idea of this story? Fill in the correct bubble.

1. Florence doesn't like to buy food.

2. There are a lot of homeless people in Florence's neighborhood.

3. Florence gets food for a homeless shelter.

4. A bakery makes fresh bread.

Reading Skill: Finding Details

> **Finding details** gives you information about people and things. We ask questions with **who, where,** or **when** to find details.
>
> **Who?** → person (Who needs help?)
>
> **Where?** → place (Where is the bakery?)
>
> **When?** → time (When does the supermarket open?)

Complete the questions with **Who, Where,** or **When.**

1. A: _____Who_____ needs help?
   B: Homeless people need help.

2. A: _____ do they live?
   B: They live in homeless shelters.

3. A: _____ does the supermarket manager throw away cans?
   B: He throws away cans in the evening.

4. A: _____ does Florence take the food?
   B: She takes the food to a homeless shelter.

5. A: _____ does Florence get bread from Fred?
   B: She gets bread from Fred every day.

Vocabulary Review

Complete the sentences. Fill in the correct bubble.

1. Florence gives food to hungry people at a _____.
   - Ⓐ bakery
   - Ⓑ supermarket
   - Ⓒ homeless shelter

2. She gets bread and cans on the same _____.
   - Ⓐ bakery
   - Ⓑ block
   - Ⓒ supermarket

3. Florence gets a lot of food from a _____.
   - Ⓐ supermarket
   - Ⓑ block
   - Ⓒ homeless shelter

4. Fred sells cakes and cookies at his _____.
   - Ⓐ bakery
   - Ⓑ bread
   - Ⓒ shelter

5. Fred also sells fresh _____.
   - Ⓐ can food
   - Ⓑ bread
   - Ⓒ cereal

Vocabulary Expansion: Learning Neighborhood Words

Learning words in groups helps you remember more words. You can learn the names of places in a neighborhood. Then, remember one or two things you do in those places. For example, you **see a doctor** at a **health clinic**.

Here are more places in Florence's neighborhood.

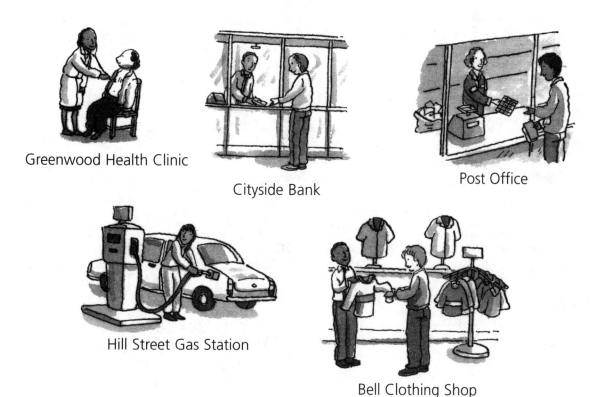

Greenwood Health Clinic

Cityside Bank

Post Office

Hill Street Gas Station

Bell Clothing Shop

1. Where do we do these things? Write the place.

Place		What we do there
Greenwood Health Clinic	⟶	see a doctor
_____	⟶	send a letter
_____	⟶	buy a sweater
_____	⟶	withdraw money
_____	⟶	fill up a car with gas

2. Add five new words from Chapter 5 to your Vocabulary Notebook on page 99.

Group Work: Talking About Stores

1. Work with a partner. Write down a store in your neighborhood where you buy each item.

Item	Store
something to drink	Al's Restaurant
a CD	
pants	
a pen	
a magazine	
shoes	
food	
your idea:	
your idea:	

2. Find a new partner. Share your answers.

Writing

Do you like to shop? Write about something you buy every week.

1. I buy a _____ every week.

2. I buy it at _____ .

3. I buy it because _____ .

Using the Internet

Do an Internet search about homeless shelters. Use a search engine like Yahoo!. Visit two Web sites or more. Tell a partner three things you learned about homeless shelters.

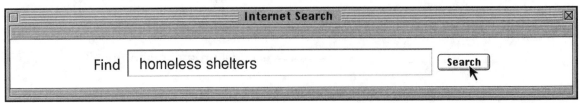

Internet Search

Find | homeless shelters | Search

1. living room   2. dining room   3. kitchen   4. bedroom   5. closet

Key Vocabulary

Complete the sentences with a word from the pictures.

   a. People cook food in the _____.

   b. People eat dinner in the _____.

   c. People usually sleep in the _____.

   d. People put clothes in a _____.

   e. People talk with friends and watch TV in the _____.

Before You Read

Look at the chapter title and the picture. Where does the story take place?
Read the story to check your guess.

  Ⓐ A hotel   **Ⓑ** A school   **Ⓒ** A house

A Home Full of Children

Louis needs a quiet place to study. He has a big math test tomorrow. He takes his math book to his **bedroom**. But he can't study there. Paul is reading to two sisters. Louis walks down the hall. He looks in the other bedrooms. He sees someone in every room. Maria is playing her flute in one room. Becky and Meghan are listening to music in another room. Mark is talking on the phone in the last bedroom.

Louis has nine brothers and seven sisters. They are all adopted. His mother always says, "Adoption puts children into loving families. Now I have 17 wonderful children to love."

Louis likes being in a big family, but today he wants to be alone. He really needs to study. He looks in the **living room**. His little brothers are watching television there. In the **dining room** Brian, Keith, and Jenny are playing cards.

Louis goes into the **kitchen**. His mother is putting away the groceries. She asks Louis to help. There are many things to put away. The family eats eight boxes of cereal each week. They use five rolls of toilet paper. They drink 14 gallons of milk.

Louis and his mother put away the groceries. Then Louis sits at the kitchen table to study. But his brothers Mike and John come into the kitchen. They need to make cookies for a Boy Scout meeting.

Louis is ready to quit. "There is no place for me to study!" he shouts. He picks up his book and leaves the kitchen.

Two hours later Louis's mother looks for him. She can't find him.

She goes into the bathroom with some clean towels. She opens the

25 **closet**. Louis is sitting on the floor. He has a flashlight in one hand. He

has his math book in his other hand.

"Look, Mama," he says. "I finally have a quiet place to study."

Comprehension

Complete the sentences. Fill in the correct bubble.

1. Louis needs to study for a _____ test.
   (A) history   (B) math   (C) English

2. Louis has _____.
   (A) nine brothers   (B) seven brothers   (C) five brothers

3. All the children in the family are _____.
   (A) boys   (B) adopted   (C) Boy Scouts

4. Each week the family drinks 14 gallons of _____.
   (A) cereal   (B) toilet paper (C) milk

5. Louis is a good _____.
   (A) student   (B) sister   (C) Boy Scout

Main Idea

What is the main idea of this story? Fill in the correct bubble.

(1) Adoption is good.

(2) Louis's brothers and sisters do not need to study.

(3) Louis must help his mother every day.

(4) Louis needs to find a quiet place to study.

Reading Skill: Understanding the Topic

Understanding the topic of a story helps you understand what the story is about. The topic is the subject or general idea of a story. To understand the topic read a story and try to say what the subject is.

Read the paragraphs. Choose the correct topic for each paragraph.

1. Louis can't study in his bedroom. His brother is reading to his sisters. He can't study in the kitchen. His brothers are making cookies. He can't study in the dining room. His brothers and sister are playing cards.

   a. Louis can't study in his bedroom.

   b. Louis can't find a quiet room to study in.

2. Maria has music lessons every week. Maria practices every day. She plays the flute in the school band. Someday Maria wants to be a famous flute player.

   a. Maria has music lessons.

   b. Maria likes playing the flute.

Vocabulary Review

Unscramble the words.

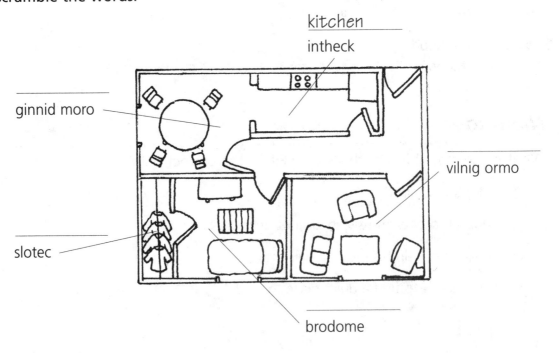

kitchen
intheck

ginnid moro

vilnig ormo

slotec

brodome

Vocabulary Expansion: Grouping Words

Grouping new words can help you remember them. One way to do this is to think of a room. Then try to remember two or three things you do in that room. For example, you **sleep**, **dress**, and **read** in a **bedroom**.

1. Look at some activities Louis's family does.

cook

eat

hang up clothes

relax

sleep

2. Where does the family do each of these things? Write an activity in each box.

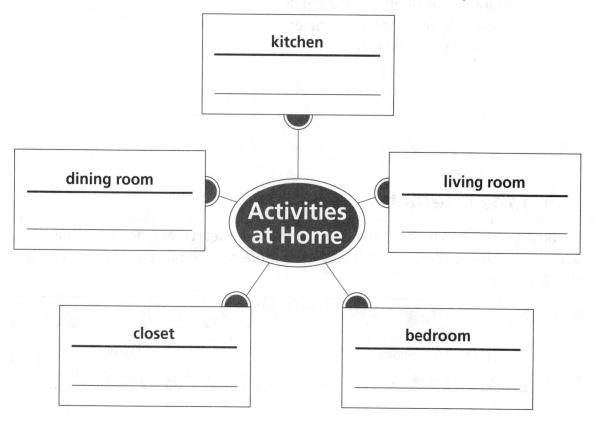

kitchen

dining room

living room

Activities at Home

closet

bedroom

3. Add five new words from Chapter 6 to your Vocabulary Notebook on page 99.

Group Work: Asking People About Home Activities

Interview five people. Ask them where they do these activities at home.
Complete the chart.

| Name | Where do you _____ at home? | | |
	study	eat	relax
Maria	in the bedroom	in the dining room	in the living room

Writing

Write three sentences about your family.
Example: There are six people in my family.
            I have one sister and two brothers.
            My sister plays the flute.

1. _____ .

2. _____ .

3. _____ .

Using the Internet

Do an Internet search about the Boy Scouts. Use a search engine like Yahoo!.
Visit two Web sites or more. Tell a partner three new things you learned about
the Boy Scouts.

Internet Search	⊠
Find	Boy Scouts	Search

CHAPTER 7

Biking Down a Volcano

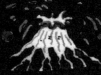

1. fishing   2. lake   3. forest   4. mountain biking   5. beach

Key Vocabulary

Complete the sentences with a word from the picture.

a. When you try to catch a fish, you are _____.

b. You can go fishing at the ocean or on a _____.

c. When you ride a bicycle up and down big hills, you are _____.

d. Many trees in one area are called a _____.

e. The _____ is where the ocean and the land meet.

Before You Read

Read the chapter title and look at the picture. What does the man want to do?
Read the story to check your guess.

(A) Go mountain biking   (B) Go fishing   (C) Go swimming

Biking Down a Volcano

Every year Valerie and Richard Benson go on a nice vacation.
Sometimes they go to the **beach**. Sometimes they go to the
mountains. Valerie's favorite sport is **fishing**, so sometimes Valerie
and Richard go to a **lake** and fish.

5   This year Richard wants to do something new. He loves riding his
bike. He wants to go **mountain biking**. Valerie doesn't like biking. She
really doesn't like riding up hills.

"I'll make a deal with you," she tells Richard. "We can go mountain
biking, but I choose the place."

10   Richard says OK. He doesn't care about the place. He just wants to
go mountain biking.

Valerie turns on her computer and logs on to the Internet. She uses
a search engine and types in two words: biking and Hawaii.

Soon Valerie finds a good Web site. It is for a biking company on
15 Maui, a Hawaiian island. This company has the perfect bike trip for
Valerie. She sends an e-mail to get more information.

See Page 11

"We are going mountain biking in Hawaii," Valerie tells Richard
at dinner. Richard is happy. He thinks about biking on the coast and in
the **forest**.

20   In Hawaii he learns the truth. Richard and Valerie are going

mountain biking, but it is all downhill! The biking company drives them to the top of a volcano called Haleakala. Then Valerie and Richard bike 38 miles down to the ocean. Both Richard and Valerie enjoy their bike ride.

"This is great!" says Richard. "Can we do it again tomorrow?"

Comprehension

True or False? Fill in the correct bubble.   **True**   **False**

1. Valerie and Richard always vacation in Hawaii. . . . . . (T) . . . . (F)

2. Richard only likes to bike downhill. . . . . (T) . . . . (F)

3. Valerie finds a good vacation place online. . . . . (T) . . . . (F)

4. Richard wants to bike down Haleakala again. . . . . . . (T) . . . . (F)

5. Valerie is good at using the Internet. . . . . (T) . . . . (F)

Main Idea

What is the main idea of this story? Fill in the correct bubble.

1. Valerie and Richard like Hawaii.

2. There's a good mountain bike company on Maui.

3. Valerie plans a good mountain bike riding trip.

4. Richard and Valerie don't like the same sports.

Reading Skill: Making Inferences

To **make an inference** you use what is *written* in a story to guess at something that is *not* written. You can understand more about the story when you make inferences.

Information from the story		Inference
Valerie finds a vacation place using the Internet.		Valerie knows how to use the Internet to find information.

1. Read the conversation.

   Richard: Let's ride our bikes to the beach.

   Valerie: We can't right now. The bikes are in the car. First, we go to the top of the volcano. Then we ride 38 miles to the bottom.

   Richard: Is the whole ride downhill?

   Valerie: Yes. It's the only way to go!

   Richard: Really? That's great!

2. Underline the best answer. Write it on the line.

   a. Richard and Valerie are ___in Hawaii___ (at home, in Hawaii).

   b. They are talking _____ (after, before) they ride down the volcano.

   c. Richard is _____ (surprised, sad) that the bike ride is all downhill.

Vocabulary Review

Complete the sentences. Write the missing word.

beach	forest	fishing	lake	mountain biking

1. Richard and Valerie like _____ down the volcano.

2. Richard likes biking and walking in the _____. He likes to look at the trees and animals.

3. Valerie and Richard's hotel is on the _____. They see the ocean from their room.

4. Valerie is very good at _____. She usually catches a lot of fish.

5. Sometimes they go fishing on a _____.

Vocabulary Expansion: Grouping Sports Words

Learning words in groups helps you remember more words. One way to do this is by learning the names of activities. Then, try to remember words used with each activity. For example, **lake**, **boat**, and **fishing pole** are used for **fishing**.

1. Study the words below. Write the correct words in the correct boxes.

mountain bike

net

fishing pole

water bottle

pump

hook

helmet

bait

waders

gloves

Fishing	Mountain Biking
fishing pole	

2. Add five new words from Chapter 7 to your Vocabulary Notebook on page 100.

Group Work: Discussing Outdoor Activities

1. Work with a partner. Read the list of outdoor activities. Tell your partner what outdoor activities you like to do. For example, "I like golf, skiing, . . ."

baseball	biking	fishing	golf
hiking	running	soccer	sailing
skiing	swimming	tennis	volleyball

2. Write activities you like in the circle on the left.
3. Write activities your partner likes in the circle on the right.
4. Write activities you both like in the middle.

Outdoor Activities

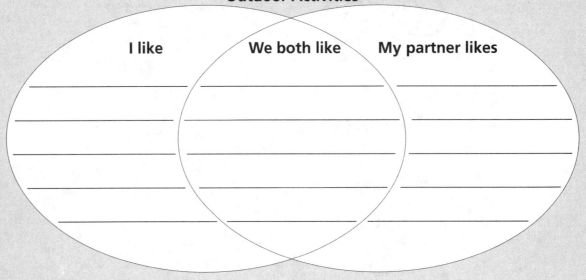

I like   We both like   My partner likes

Writing

Write about an outdoor activity you like.

1. I like _____ .

2. I like it because _____ .

3. I do this activity with _____ .
   (name of person)

Using the Internet

Do an Internet search on three vacation places you want to visit. Use a search engine like Yahoo!. Tell a partner one thing about each place you want to visit.

Internet Search ☒
Find   Hawaii   [Search]

CHAPTER 8

The Flood

1. rain   2. river   3. flood   4. scared   5. safe

Key Vocabulary

Complete the sentences with a word from the picture.

a. When water comes down from the sky, it is called _____.

b. When it rains a lot, the _____ has too much water.

c. When the river has too much water, there is a _____.

d. When there is a flood, it is dangerous. People are _____.

e. The people inside the building are warm and _____.

Before You Read

Read the chapter title and look at the picture. Why is the man outside in the rain? Read the story to check your guess.

(A) He is having fun.   (B) He is working.   (C) He is in a flood.

The Flood

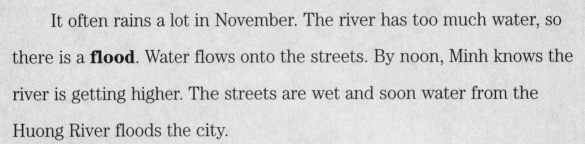

See Page 116

"I don't like this **rain**," says Minh Tran. "November rain is sometimes dangerous. But we are not close to the **river**. We are **safe** here."

Minh is a tour guide in Vietnam. He is traveling with 15 tourists. Minh's job is to show them the city of Hue, but he can't. There is too
5   much rain. Minh and the tourists stay inside their hotel.

It often rains a lot in November. The river has too much water, so there is a **flood**. Water flows onto the streets. By noon, Minh knows the river is getting higher. The streets are wet and soon water from the Huong River floods the city.

10   "What can we do?" asks one of the tourists.

"We must stay here," says Minh. "We can't leave. All of the roads are underwater."

The tourists look **scared**. Minh smiles and tells them again that the hotel is safe.

15   "It is not dangerous here," he tells the tourists. "Please enjoy a quiet day inside."

At 5:00 p.m. there is three feet of water in the streets. Minh and the tourists are safe, but other people are in danger. Some people run to the hotel. They bring blankets and sleep on the floor. That night Minh talks
20   to them.

"I remember one year. It rained for weeks," says an old man. "The whole city was underwater, and my family was very scared. We ran to this hotel. Everyone was hungry. People needed food, and I wanted to help. I decided to swim through town. I looked in the empty houses."

"What did you see?" asks Minh.

"I saw a chicken in one house. I saw potatoes in another house,"
25 says the old man. "I took them and came back to the hotel."

"I don't think you need to do that this time," says Minh.

"Don't worry," the old man says. "This time I am prepared." He
opens his bag. Inside are oranges, fish, and rice.

Luckily, the rain stops. The next morning, the streets start to dry.
30 Minh and the tourists are ready to leave. Minh waves goodbye to the old
man. The man smiles and gives Minh an orange.

"Here," he says. "For the next flood!"

Comprehension

True or False? Fill in the correct bubble.   **True**   **False**

1. Minh is a tour guide. . . . . ⓣ . . . . Ⓕ

2. In November it rains a lot in Hue. . . . . ⓣ . . . . Ⓕ

3. People come to the hotel to sleep on the floor. . . . . . ⓣ . . . . Ⓕ

4. The old man has potatoes in his bag. . . . . ⓣ . . . . Ⓕ

5. Minh is scared. . . . . ⓣ . . . . Ⓕ

Main Idea

What is the main idea of this story? Fill in the correct bubble.

① Minh meets an old man during a flood.

② Minh can't do his job.

③ An old man teaches Minh how to swim.

④ There is a good hotel in Hue.

Reading Skill: Understanding the Topic

Understanding the topic of a story helps you understand what the story is about. The topic is the subject or general idea of a story. To understand the topic, read a story and try to say what the subject is.

Read the paragraphs. Choose the correct topic for each paragraph.

1. It rains outside. Minh and the tourists stay inside all day. Some tourists go to their rooms and sleep. Some tourists go to the restaurant for lunch. Some play cards. Minh walks around. He makes sure everyone feels safe.

    a. Things to do at a hotel on a rainy day

    b. Things the tourists do in Vietnam

    c. Things Minh and the tourists do in the hotel on a rainy day

2. The old man tells Minh about his family. His son lives in Hanoi. He is a taxi driver. His daughter lives in Da Nang. She is a teacher. His wife died four years ago.

    a. The old man's family

    b. Cities in Vietnam

    c. The old man's son

Vocabulary Review

Complete the sentences. Fill in the correct bubble.

1. The hotel is on a hill. The hotel is _____ and dry inside.
    Ⓐ river   Ⓑ safe   Ⓒ scared

2. It rains for many days. The _____ has too much water.
    Ⓐ safe   Ⓑ river   Ⓒ tourist

3. The dog went out in the _____. Now it is wet.
    Ⓐ rain   Ⓑ hotel   Ⓒ city

4. It rained for many days. Then there was a _____ in Hue.
    Ⓐ flood   Ⓑ dry   Ⓒ swim

5. People run to the hotel. They feel _____ outside, but safe in the hotel.
    Ⓐ city   Ⓑ happy   Ⓒ scared

Vocabulary Expansion: Learning Opposite Pairs

Learning words in pairs helps you remember both words. You can learn a pair of words that have opposite meanings. For example, **safe** is the opposite of **dangerous**.

1. Match the opposites.

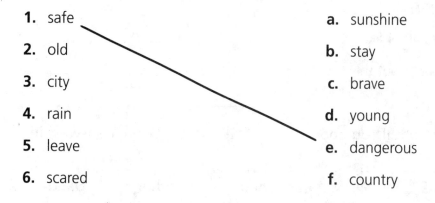

1.	safe		**a.**	sunshine
2.	old		**b.**	stay
3.	city		**c.**	brave
4.	rain		**d.**	young
5.	leave		**e.**	dangerous
6.	scared		**f.**	country

2. Work with a partner. Write more pairs of opposites.

1. _____good_____ and _____bad_____
2. _____ and _____
3. _____ and _____
4. _____ and _____
5. _____ and _____

3. Add five new words from Chapter 8 to your Vocabulary Notebook on page 100.

Group Work: Sharing Vacation Stories

1. Think about a good vacation you went on.

2. Write answers to the questions.

   - Where did you go? _____

   - Who did you go with? _____

   - When did you go? _____

   - What was the weather like? _____

   - What did you like about this vacation?
   _____

3. Ask three people to tell you about their vacations. Write their answers in the boxes.

Name	Where	Who	When	Weather	Liked
Minh	Hue, Vietnam	tourists	November	rain	talking to an old man

Writing

Write about the city or town you live in.

1. I live in _____.

2. One thing I like about my city or town is _____.

3. One thing I do not like about my city or town is _____.

Using the Internet

Do an Internet search about Vietnam. Use a search engine like Yahoo!. Visit two Web sites or more. Tell a partner three new things you learned about Vietnam.

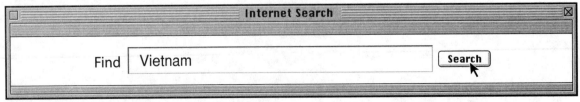

Internet Search

Find   Vietnam   [Search]

CHAPTER 9

First Day of School

1. classroom   2. cafeteria   3. principal   4. main office   5. locker

Key Vocabulary

Complete the sentences with a word from the pictures.

a. The teacher teaches his students in a _____ .

b. The student puts her jacket in a _____ .

c. Students eat in the _____ .

d. The leader of a school is called the _____ .

e. The principal's office is in the _____ .

Before You Read

Look at the chapter title and the picture. There is a boy in the principal's office. Why is he there? Read the story to check your guess.

(A) He did something bad.   (B) He is a new student.   (C) He is sick.

First Day of School

See Page 116

Lon Sampon sees a big sign over the door. It says Roosevelt High School. Lon's heart beats faster. He is scared. Today is his first day at an American high school. Lon is from Cambodia. His family just moved to California. Lon studied English in Cambodia, and he knows many

5 English words. He is still worried. Does he know enough English? Can he make friends?

Lon walks into the school. It is bigger than his school in Cambodia. Everything looks strange. He does not see any other Cambodians. The students walk past him. They all know where to go.

10 "I don't know where to go," he thinks. "I am lost already." Then he sees the **main office**, so he goes in.

A woman walks over to Lon. "Good morning," she says. "I am the **principal**, Mrs. Smith. Can I help you?"

"Yes," says Lon. "My name is Lon Sampon. I am a new student."

15 "I am pleased to meet you, Lon. Please come with me."

They go into her office. "Here," she says. She gives Lon a piece of paper. It is his class schedule.

"There are two important numbers on your schedule. The first is 104. That is the number of your homeroom," Mrs. Smith says. "It is the

20 first **classroom** you go to every morning. It is down the hall. The second number is 78 and this is your **locker** number. Your locker is next to your homeroom. You can keep your books and jacket in your locker."

Lon thanks Mrs. Smith and goes to his locker. A boy is standing next to Lon's locker.

"Hi," says the boy. "My name is Hernando. My locker is next to

25 yours."

"Hi," says Lon.

"I know you are new here," says Hernando. "The first day at a new school is difficult. Do you want to meet me in the **cafeteria** for lunch?"

Suddenly Lon feels better. Hernando seems nice, so Lon smiles.

30 "Thank you," he says. "How do you know I need help?"

Hernando laughs. "I was born in Mexico," he says. "Last year, I was the new student here."

Comprehension

True or False? Fill in the correct bubble.   **True**   **False**

1. Roosevelt High School is in California. . . . .(T) . . . . . . (F)

2. Lon Sampon is from Cambodia. . . . .(T) . . . . . . (F)

3. The principal's office is in the cafeteria. . . . .(T) . . . . . . (F)

4. Lon's homeroom is Room 78. . . . .(T) . . . . . . (F)

5. Lon will probably study English at his new school. . . .(T) . . . . . . (F)

Main Idea

What is the main idea of this story? Fill in the correct bubble.

(1) Lon starts his first day at a new school.

(2) Principals are happy to meet new students.

(3) Many students come from other countries.

(4) Hernando is a nice person.

Reading Skill: Putting Events in Order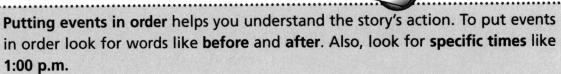

> **Putting events in order** helps you understand the story's action. To put events in order look for words like **before** and **after**. Also, look for **specific times** like **1:00 p.m.**

Put the events in the right order. Write the correct number on each line.

___1___ Lon goes to his homeroom class.

_____ **At 1:00 p.m.** Lon goes to his English class.

_____ Hernando and Lon eat lunch in the cafeteria **before** English class.

_____ **At 10:00 a.m.** Lon has math.

_____ **After** school Lon and Hernando walk home together.

Vocabulary Review

Complete the sentences. Write the missing words.

cafeteria	classroom	locker	main office	principal

1. Lon's homeroom is also a math _____.

2. The _____ works hard as the director of the school.

3. After school Lon takes his jacket out of his _____.

4. The _____ serves hot dogs and french fries on Mondays.

5. Lon goes to the _____ to see the principal.

Vocabulary Expansion: Grouping School Words

Grouping new words can help you remember them. One way to do this is to think of a room. Then, try to remember two or three things in that room. For example, **desks**, **chairs**, and a **blackboard** are all things in a **classroom**.

1. Where do you find these things at school? Fill in each box with the correct place from the map.

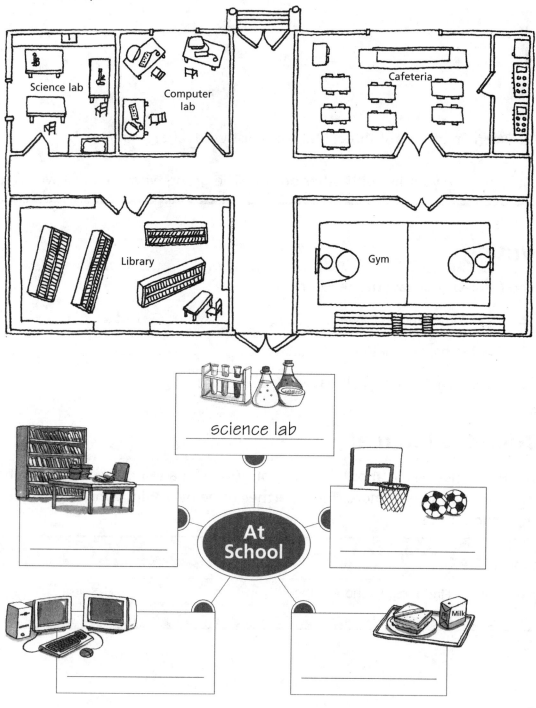

2. Add five new words from Chapter 9 to your Vocabulary Notebook on page 101.

Group Work: Talking About Your Classroom

1. Write down 10 or more things in your classroom.

Things in My Classroom

1. _desks_
2.
3.
4.
5.

6.
7.
8.
9.
10.

2. Work in groups of three. Make one list with all of your words.

3. Compare your list with other groups. The group with the most words wins.

Writing

Who (is/was) your favorite teacher?

1. My favorite teacher (is/was) _____.

2. This teacher (teaches/taught) _____.

3. I (like/liked) this teacher because _____.

 ## Using the Internet

Do an Internet search about high school clubs. Use a search engine like Yahoo!. Visit two Web sites or more. Tell a partner three new things you learned about high school clubs.

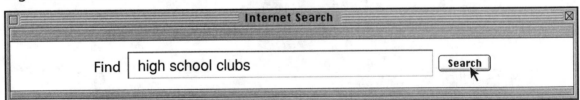

Internet Search

Find | high school clubs | Search

CHAPTER 10

Grandmother's Bear Paw Soup

Key Vocabulary

Match the sentences to the items in the picture.

a. **Mushrooms** grow in wet, dark places. ___4___

b. Cooks put **spices** in food to add special tastes. _____

c. Cooking directions are called **recipes**. _____

d. A skilled cook is called a **chef**. _____

e. You can use water, chicken, and carrots to make **soup**. _____

Before You Read

Look at the chapter title and the picture. Where are the people? Read the story to check your guess.

Ⓐ At a food festival   Ⓑ At a restaurant   Ⓒ At home

Grandmother's Bear Paw Soup

Fang Yin Chen remembers her grandmother's special **soup**. "It tasted great," she says. "My grandmother put many **spices** in it. I am a good cook, and I try to make the same soup. My soup is good, but it is not as good as my grandmother's."

5 "Why not?" asks a friend.

"I don't know," Ms. Chen says. "Something is missing."

Ms. Chen lives in Taipei, Taiwan. Every year Taipei has a big festival called the Taipei Chinese Food Festival. Thousands of people go. They go to taste the delicious food and learn new **recipes**.

See Page 116

10 This year the Taiwanese festival has a lot of **chefs** from Shanghai. Ms. Chen's grandmother was born in Shanghai, so Ms. Chen decides to go to the festival. "Maybe one of the chefs can help me fix my soup," she thinks.

The festival is at the Taipei World Trade Center. Ms. Chen walks
15 through many rooms. One room has food made with **mushrooms**. Another room has many noodle dishes. There is even a room for snack foods.

Ms. Chen finds the room for food from Shanghai. It is full of wonderful food. Some of the recipes are 1,500 years old. Ms. Chen tells a
20 chef about her grandmother's soup. The chef smiles and nods his head.

"I think I know why your soup tastes different," he says. "Your grandmother probably put bear paw in her soup. My grandmother did the same thing. But now people do not like the idea of killing and eating bears."

25 "Oh!" says Ms. Chen. "Then I can't make my grandmother's soup."

The chef smiles. "Yes, you can. You do not need bear paws," he says. "You can use beef with special spices instead." The chef gives Ms. Chen a piece of paper. "Try this recipe," he says.

Ms. Chen thanks the chef. The next day, she tries the new recipe. It 30 tastes great! Now her soup *does* taste like her grandmother's soup. Ms. Chen can't wait to make the soup for her parents.

Comprehension

True or False? Fill in the correct bubble.	True	False
1. Ms. Chen works at the food festival.	T	F
2. She lives in Shanghai.	T	F
3. Some recipes from China are 1,500 years old.	T	F
4. Today most people do not like eating bear paws.	T	F
5. Ms. Chen likes to cook.	T	F

Main Idea

What is the main idea of this story? Fill in the correct bubble.

1. The Taipei Chinese Food Festival is very popular.

2. Ms. Chen goes to a food festival to ask about her grandmother's soup recipe.

3. Ms. Chen is a good chef.

4. Food from Shanghai is hard to make.

Reading Skill: Identifying Cause and Effect

Identifying cause and effect helps you see connections. A **cause** makes something happen. An **effect** is what happens.

Cause
The chef tastes the soup.
It is OK, but not great.

Effect
The chef adds spices to the soup.

Match the **cause** and the **effect**.

Cause	Effect
1. Some people want to try new and different food.	**a.** He gives her a new recipe.
2. Ms. Chen wants her soup to taste like her grandmother's soup.	**b.** She says, "Then I can't make my grandmother's soup."
3. The chef wants to help Ms. Chen.	**c.** They go to food festivals.
4. Ms. Chen can't get bear paws for her soup.	**d.** She can't wait to make the soup for her parents.
5. Ms. Chen learns to make the soup without bear paws.	**e.** She goes to the food festival.

Vocabulary Review

Complete the sentences. Fill in the correct bubble.

1. Recipes are _____ for making food.
    (A) directions   (B) food   (C) bear paws

2. Ms. Chen's grandmother's **soup** was a special _____.
    (A) mushroom   (B) beef   (C) recipe

3. A **chef**'s job is to _____ food.
    (A) eat   (B) cook   (C) sniff

4. Ms. Chen put **spices** in her soup to make it _____ better.
    (A) look   (B) feel   (C) taste

5. Mushrooms are a good _____ to put in soup.
    (A) rice   (B) meat   (C) food

Vocabulary Expansion: Grouping Food Words

Putting words in groups makes it easier to remember them. Food comes in many different kinds of groups. For example: **apples, bananas,** and **oranges** are all **fruit** words.

1. Study the pictures of six food groups.

Six Food Groups

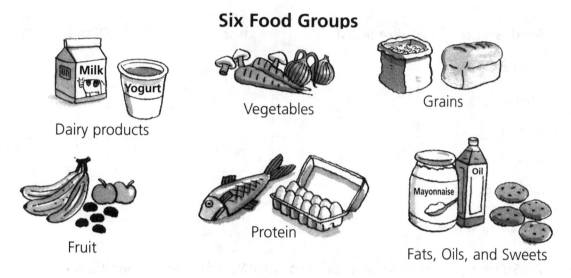

Dairy products

Vegetables

Grains

Fruit

Protein

Fats, Oils, and Sweets

2. Write the food group names on the lines.

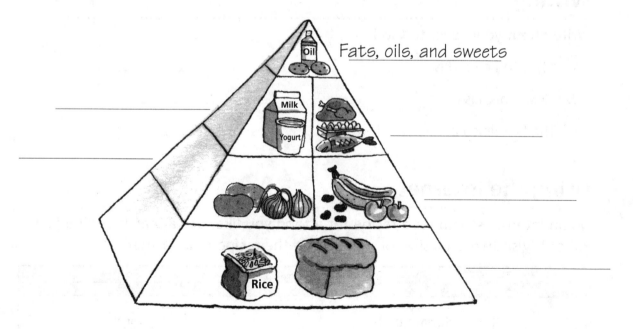

Fats, oils, and sweets

3. Add five new words from Chapter 10 to your Vocabulary Notebook on page 101.

Group Work: Planning a Menu

1. Work in groups of three. Plan a menu for one day. Make sure that each meal has one dairy product, one grain, one protein, one fruit, one vegetable, and one food with fat or oil.

_____, _____, and _____'s Menu
  (Name)   (Name)   (Name)

Food Group	Breakfast	Lunch	Dinner
Dairy Products			
Grains			
Protein			
Fruit			
Vegetables			
Fats, Oils, and Sweets			

2. Share your menu with another group. Which menu is healthier?

Writing

Write about your favorite food.

1. My favorite food is _____.

2. I like it because _____.

3. The first time I ate this food was _____.

Using the Internet

Do an Internet search for a recipe for a food you like. Use a search engine like Yahoo!. Visit two Web sites or more. Read the recipe to a partner.

Internet Search	☒
Find chicken curry	Search

CHAPTER 11

Golfing in a Storm

Key Vocabulary

Match the sentences to the items in the picture.

a. Tree branches blow in the **wind**. __2__

b. When it rains, the **clouds** are dark. _____

c. The bright flash in the sky is **lightning**. _____

d. **Thunder** is the sound that comes after lightning. _____

e. The **sun** gives us light and heat. _____

Before You Read

Look at the chapter title and the picture. What do you think the story is about?
Read the story to check your guess.

- Ⓐ A man and a boy watching a lightning storm
- Ⓑ A man being hurt by lightning
- Ⓒ A man and a boy golfing

Golfing in a Storm

Young-Woo Kim loved golf. He played in all kinds of weather. Heat didn't stop him. Cold didn't stop him. **Wind** and **rain** didn't stop him. The only thing that stopped Mr. Kim's golf game was **lightning**. Golfers are afraid of lightning. They know a golf course is a dangerous place during a

5 lightning storm. When lightning comes, golf course workers blow a loud horn. The horn tells everyone to stop playing and get inside.

One day Mr. Kim played golf near his home in Seoul, Korea. He played with his son Jong-Chul. They finished 17 holes. Then they walked to the last hole, the 18th hole. Mr. Kim was happy. He had a low score.

10 Jong-Chul was happy, too. "I am playing well today," he told his father.

See Page 11

Mr. Kim looked up at the sky. The **clouds** were dark. A few raindrops fell. Mr. Kim saw lightning. He heard **thunder**. The thunder sounded far away, but Mr. Kim was afraid.

"We need to go," Mr. Kim said. "It is dangerous to be out here in a

15 lightning storm."

"I know," said Jong-Chul. "But we are almost at the end. We have only one more hole to play."

Just then Mr. Kim and Jong-Chul saw lightning again. This time it was close. They heard the golf course horn.

20 "Okay," said Jong-Chul. "You're right. Let's go inside."

But they were not fast enough. The next flash of lightning came right toward Mr. Kim. It knocked him to the ground.

Mr. Kim woke up in the hospital. He said to Jong-Chul, "I saw a bright
25 light. I didn't hear the thunder. I only saw the light. For a minute, I thought
I was dead."

But Mr. Kim was lucky. The lightning didn't kill him. It made a hole in
his shirt. It made another hole in his pants.

Mr. Kim's left arm was burned. His left leg was burned, too. But the
30 burns weren't bad. Mr. Kim spent only one night in the hospital. Five days
later, he and Jong-Chul played golf again. This time they were careful.
When they started to play the **sun** was out. But later they saw dark clouds,
and they knew what to do. They left the golf course right away.

Comprehension

True or False? Fill in the correct bubble.   **True**   **False**

1. Mr. Kim doesn't play golf when it's cold. . . . . (T) . . . . (F)

2. Jong-Chul played well. . . . . (T) . . . . (F)

3. Jong-Chul wanted to stay and finish the game. . . . . . (T) . . . . (F)

4. The lightning hit Jong-Chul. . . . . (T) . . . . (F)

5. A good golf score is a low score. . . . . (T) . . . . (F)

Main Idea

What is the main idea of this story? Fill in the correct bubble.

1. Families are happy when they do things together.

2. Mr. Kim likes to play golf with his son.

3. Lightning can kill a person.

4. Mr. Kim is hit by lightning while playing golf.

Reading Skill: Finding Details

Finding details helps you understand a story better. We ask questions with
who, **where**, or **when** to find details about a reading.

Who? → person	(Who is hit by lightning?)
Where? → place	(Where does Mr. Kim live?)
What? → thing	(What does Mr. Kim love to play?)

1. Find details to answer the questions.

   a. Who had a low score? _____Mr. Kim did._____

   b. Who was hit by lightning? _____

   c. Where is the golf course? _____

   d. Where was Mr. Kim burned? _____

   e. What hit Mr. Kim? _____

   f. What does Jong-Chul play with his father? _____

2. Write three more questions about the story.

   a. Who played golf? _____

   b. Where _____ ?

   c. What _____ ?

3. Ask a partner your questions.

Vocabulary Review

Complete the sentences. Write the missing word.

clouds	lightning	sun	thunder	wind

1. It is hot because the _____ is shining.

2. The sky was blue. But now it is full of dark _____ .

3. Jong-Chul hears _____ . A storm is coming.

4. Mr. Kim sees a lot of _____ during the storm.

5. Leaves on the trees move when the _____ blows.

Vocabulary Expansion: Describing the Weather

Weather words like **rain** and **wind** are nouns. To describe the weather, we use the adjective form of these words like **rainy** and **windy**. For example, when **the wind is blowing**, we say it's **windy**.

1. Study the words in the box.

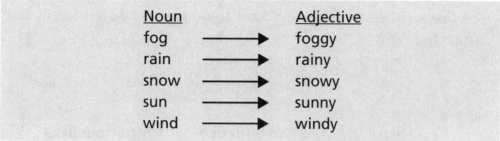

Noun		Adjective
fog	⟶	foggy
rain	⟶	rainy
snow	⟶	snowy
sun	⟶	sunny
wind	⟶	windy

2. Write a short sentence under each picture.

It's windy.

3. Add five new words from Chapter 11 to your Vocabulary Notebook on page 102.

Group Work: Talking About Family Activities

Young-Woo and Jong-Chul Kim like to play golf together. Jong-Chul also likes to read to his little sister. He likes to play cards with his whole family, too.

What are some activities you like to do with your family?

1. Work with a partner. Write five activities you like to do with your family in the circle on the left.
2. Write five activities your partner likes to do with his or her family in the circle on the right.
3. Write five activities you both like to do in the middle.

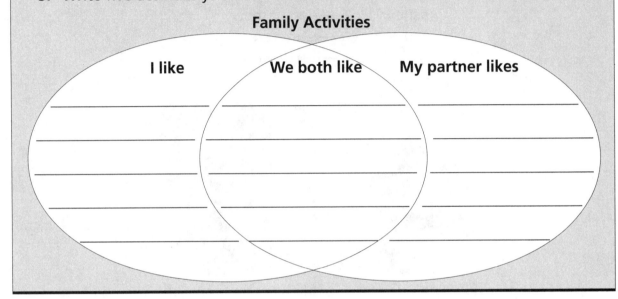

Family Activities

I like   We both like   My partner likes

Writing

What is your favorite season: winter, spring, summer or fall? Why?

1. My favorite season is _____.

2. I like this season because _____.

3. I also like this season because _____.

Using the Internet

Do an Internet search about the weather in your favorite city (Example: Tokyo, London, Sydney). Use a search engine like Yahoo!. Visit two Web sites or more. Tell a partner about the weather for tomorrow.

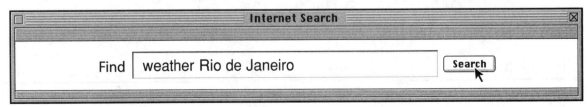

Internet Search

Find   weather Rio de Janeiro   Search

CHAPTER **12**

Lost on a Mountain

Key Vocabulary

Match the sentences to the items in the picture.

a. Carry your **backpack** on your back. __1__

b. Blow your **whistle** when you are lost. _____

c. Wear **gloves** to keep your hands warm. _____

d. Wear good shoes and **socks** to keep your feet warm. _____

e. Wear a **raincoat** to keep dry. _____

Before You Read

Look at the chapter title and the picture. Where is the woman going? Read the story to check your guess.

She is going on _____.

Ⓐ a car trip   Ⓑ a vacation   Ⓒ a hike

Lost on a Mountain

See Page 117

Abby Brown knows how dangerous Mount Washington in New Hampshire can be. Almost every year someone dies on the mountain. There are a lot of storms. The weather can get very cold very quickly. "I must be careful," Abby thinks.

5   She wants to hike up and down the mountain in one day. It should take her seven hours. She packs a lot of clothes for the hike. First, she puts a sweater and extra **socks** in her **backpack**. She also packs a **raincoat** and **gloves**. Then, she packs fruit and water. Finally, she puts a **whistle** in her pocket.

10   Abby wears a T-shirt and shorts. She starts hiking up the mountain. The weather is warm and sunny. Abby loves the beautiful trees. She meets many hikers. They smile and say hello.

      After two hours, things are different. The tall trees are gone. Abby sees only rocks and small plants. The wind blows. It is colder. Abby puts

15 on her sweater and socks. In an hour she gets to the top. "I'm here!" she says.

      Abby doesn't stay at the top. The weather is bad. It is very foggy and Abby can't see very well. Soon she is lost. She yells for help. No one answers, so she yells and yells again. Then Abby remembers her whistle.

20 The whistle makes a loud sound. She blows the whistle hard but still

no one answers. Again and again Abby blows the whistle.

Finally, she hears someone. Abby looks and sees a park ranger, a man who works on the mountain. He waves to Abby.

"Wow," she says. "I'm happy to see you."

Comprehension

Complete the sentences. Fill in the correct bubble.

1. It should take Abby _____ to hike up and down Mount Washington.
   - (A) an hour
   - (B) five hours
   - (C) seven hours

2. Abby takes food, a whistle, and _____.
   - (A) a sweater
   - (B) a friend
   - (C) an aspirin

3. The weather at the top of the mountain is _____.
   - (A) good
   - (B) sunny
   - (C) foggy

4. Abby uses her whistle to _____.
   - (A) call for help
   - (B) play a song
   - (C) get warm

5. The _____ can change fast at the top of a mountain.
   - (A) people
   - (B) weather
   - (C) clothes

Main Idea

What is the main idea of this story? Fill in the correct bubble.

1. Abby takes a hike on Mount Washington but gets lost.

2. People should not hike alone.

3. The weather changes quickly on Mount Washington.

4. Abby needs more friends.

Reading Skill: Putting Events in Order

Putting events in order helps you understand the story's action.

Put the events in order. Write the correct number on each line.

_____ She gets lost.

_____ She says hello to many hikers.

___1___ Abby puts fruit and water in her backpack.

_____ She sees a park ranger.

_____ She starts hiking up Mount Washington.

_____ She puts on a sweater and extra socks.

Vocabulary Review

Complete the sentences. Write the missing word.

backpack	gloves	raincoat	socks	whistle

1. Abby gets ready for her hike. She puts things in her _____.

2. Abby's hands get cold. She puts on a pair of _____.

3. It starts to rain. Abby puts on a _____.

4. Her feet are cold. Abby puts on extra _____.

5. Abby is lost. She blows her _____ for help.

Vocabulary Expansion: Learning *A* and *A Pair Of*

We use the expression **a pair of** for clothes that have two parts. For example, we say **a pair of** gloves. For clothes that are only one item, we usually use **a**. For example, we say **a** hat.

1. Write the clothes we use with **a** in the left circle. Write the clothes we use with **a pair of** in the right circle.

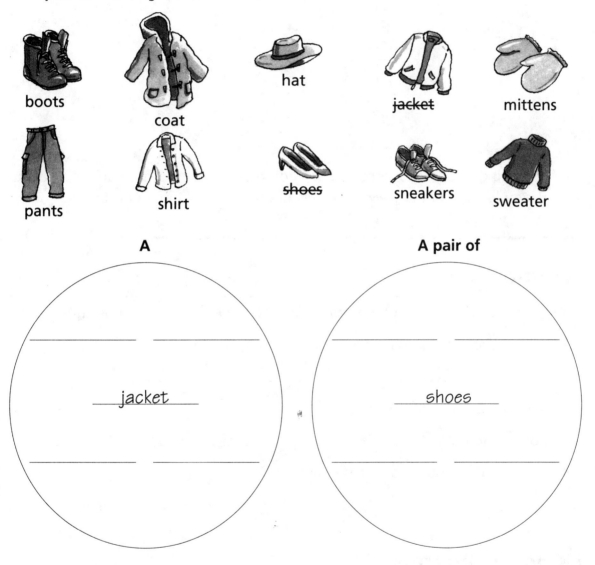

A   **A pair of**

_____   _____   _____   _____

_____jacket_____   _____shoes_____

_____   _____   _____   _____

2. Add five new words from Chapter 12 to your Vocabulary Notebook on page 102.

Group Work: Choosing Clothes for a Trip

1. Think of a place you want to visit. Write the clothes you need for the trip.

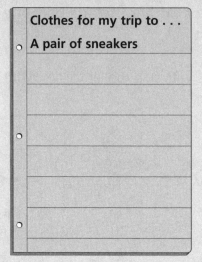

Clothes for my trip to . . .

A pair of sneakers

2. In small groups, say where you are going and what clothes you are taking. Example: "I'm going to Mount Washington. I'm taking a pair of sneakers, . . ."

Writing

Abby wants to visit your city or town next week. Write answers to her questions.

1. Abby: What clothes do I bring?

   You: Bring _____.

2. Abby: What can I do in your town?

   You: You can _____.

3. Abby: What is your favorite restaurant?

   You: _____.

Using the Internet

Do an Internet search on clothing stores in a city you want to visit (Example: Chicago, Hong Kong, or Paris). Use a search engine like Yahoo!. Visit two Web sites or more. Tell a partner the names of the city and three clothing stores there.

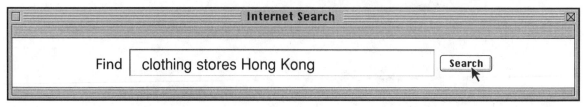

Internet Search

Find | clothing stores Hong Kong | Search

CHAPTER 13

A Cat Saves a Family

1. backyard   2. stairs   3. stove   4. refrigerator   5. bed

Key Vocabulary

Complete the sentences with a word from the pictures.

a. Food is cooked on a _____.

b. People keep food cold in the _____.

c. People like to sit outside in the _____.

d. People sleep in a _____.

e. The cat goes up the _____ to get to the second floor.

Before You Read

Look at the chapter title and the picture. What is the cat doing? Read the story to check your guess.

(A) Waking up the girl   (B) Playing with the girl   (C) Going to sleep

A Cat Saves a Family

Debbie Henderson's cat is all black with a white face and small white feet. He looks like he is wearing socks, so Debbie named him Socks. Socks is a friendly cat. He loves to rub against people's legs. Debbie loves her cat. She always gives him water and good food. She
5 likes to play with him when she gets home from school. Debbie and Socks spend a lot of time in their **backyard**.

When Debbie got Socks, he had one habit Debbie didn't like. He liked to sleep on Debbie's **bed**. Every night Socks curled up next to her. At first she thought it was funny. But soon she didn't like it. "The bed is
10 not big enough for both of us," Debbie said.

Debbie wanted Socks off the bed. She got a nice big box. She put a soft blanket in it. She put the box in the kitchen next to the **refrigerator**. Every evening Debbie put Socks in the box, but every evening Socks jumped out. He climbed the **stairs** and he jumped into
15 bed with Debbie. Every evening Debbie carried Socks back to the kitchen.

Finally, Socks gave up. He stayed in his box. For three months Socks didn't go up to the bedroom at night. Then one night he came into the bedroom again. He jumped on the bed, and Debbie woke up. "Not
20 again," she said.

But this time Socks acted strange. He didn't lie down and go to sleep. Instead, Socks meowed loudly. "What's wrong with you?" asked Debbie.

Then Debbie smelled smoke. She ran downstairs. The kitchen

25 **stove** was on fire. Quickly Debbie woke her parents up. They called the fire department. Then Debbie and her parents ran out of the house. Debbie carried Socks in her arms. Soon firefighters came and they put out the fire. The fire burned most of the kitchen. But it did not burn the rest of the house.

30 "Socks saved us!" said Debbie. "He knew the house was on fire. He came to warn us!"

"It's true," Debbie's mother said. "Socks saved our lives."

Comprehension

True or False? Fill in the correct bubble.

1. The cat's name is Socks because he plays with socks. . T . . . . . . F

2. Debbie doesn't want Socks to sleep on her bed. . . . . T . . . . . . F

3. Socks learned to sleep in his box. . . . . T . . . . . . F

4. Socks woke Debbie's parents up. . . . . T . . . . . . F

5. Debbie and her parents think Socks is a smart cat. . . . T . . . . . . F

Main Idea

What is the main idea of this story? Fill in the correct bubble.

(1) You should check your stove before you go to bed.

(2) It's smart to have a cat.

(3) Debbie and Socks like to play in the backyard.

(4) Socks saves Debbie and her parents from a fire.

Reading Skill: Identifying Cause and Effect

Identifying **cause and effect** helps you see connections. A **cause** makes something happen. An **effect** is what happens. We can use the word **so** to connect the cause and the effect.

Cause
Socks is thirsty,

Effect
so Debbie gives him water.

Match the **cause** and the **effect**.

Cause	**Effect**
1. The cat is black with white paws,	**a.** so she makes a bed for him in the kitchen.
2. Debbie doesn't want Socks to sleep in her bed,	**b.** so Debbie's parents call the fire department.
3. Socks sleeps in the kitchen,	**c.** so she wakes up her parents.
4. Debbie smells smoke,	**d.** so Debbie names him Socks.
5. There is a fire in the kitchen,	**e.** so Debbie is surprised to see Socks jump on her bed.

Vocabulary Review

Complete the sentences. Fill in the correct bubble.

1. Socks likes to go up the _____ to Debbie's bedroom.
   - (A) stairs
   - (B) closet
   - (C) stove

2. Debbie takes water out of the _____ to give to Socks.
   - (A) stove
   - (B) refrigerator
   - (C) bed

3. Debbie and Socks play in the _____.
   - (A) refrigerator
   - (B) backyard
   - (C) stove

4. Debbie makes Socks a soft _____ to sleep in.
   - (A) backyard
   - (B) refrigerator
   - (C) bed

5. Debbie's mother cooks dinner on the _____.
   - (A) refrigerator
   - (B) stairs
   - (C) stove

Vocabulary Expansion: Grouping Household Words

Putting new words in groups can help you remember them. For example, a **bed**, a **desk**, and a **nightstand** are all things found in a **bedroom**.

1. Look at the pictures. Write the words in the correct circles below.

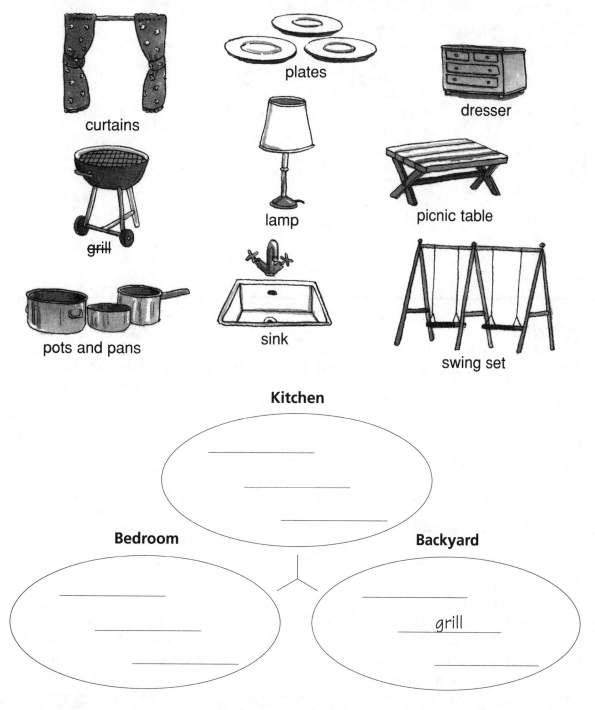

curtains

plates

dresser

grill

lamp

picnic table

pots and pans

sink

swing set

Kitchen

_____

_____

_____

Bedroom

_____

_____

_____

Backyard

_____

grill

_____

2. Add five new words from Chapter 13 to your Vocabulary Notebook on page 103.

Group Work: Talking About Homes

Interview five people. Ask them two things they like about their home and one thing they dislike (do not like) about their home.
For example:

A: What do you like about your home?
B: I like the safe neighborhood and the nice backyard.
A: What do you dislike about your home?
B: I dislike the small kitchen.

Name	Like #1	Like #2	Dislike
Mr. Henderson	safe neighborhood	nice backyard	small kitchen

Writing

Answer the questions about your bedroom. Write complete sentences.

1. What color is your bedroom?

_____.

2. What furniture do you have in your bedroom?

_____.

3. What do you like best about your bedroom?

_____.

Using the Internet

Do an Internet search about renting a house or apartment in your city or town. Use a search engine like Yahoo!. Visit two Web sites or more. Tell a partner about three places you like.

Internet Search	☒

Find | apartments San Francisco | **Search**

CHAPTER 14

Robot Wrestling

1. computer   2. robot   3. battery   4. remote control   5. screen

Key Vocabulary

Complete the sentences with a word from the picture.

a. The _____ gives the robot power.

b. The boy's _____ is a machine made from cans, a cooking pot, and computer chips.

c. He uses the _____ to make the robot move.

d. The boy uses a _____ to send e-mail messages and find information on the Internet.

e. He reads his e-mail messages on his computer _____ .

Before You Read

Look at the chapter title and the picture. Why is the boy using the computer? Read the story to check your guess.

(A) To do his homework   (B) To build his robot   (C) To play a game

Robot Wrestling

See Page 116

Toshiki Uno is 15 and lives in Tokyo, Japan. He thought his **robot** was the right size, but he wanted to be sure. So Toshiki turned on his **computer**. He logged on to the robot sumo Web site. He read the information he needed on the **screen**.

5   "Good," he said to his friend Hiro. "My robot is the perfect size. Its sides are 18 centimeters long. And it weighs two kilograms."

"When did you build it?" asked Hiro.

"I started work on it two months ago. I worked every day after school. I used pieces of a cooking pot and tin cans, too. I put in a

10   **battery** and computer chips. I have a **remote control** to move the robot fast or slow."

Toshiki named his robot Power Robot. He entered it in the All Japan Robot Sumo Tournament. On December 22, he took Power Robot to the tournament in Tokyo. Hiro went with him. They saw high school

15   students and adults from all across Japan. Most people had a homemade robot. They all wanted to win the tournament.

"Tell me again how this tournament works," said Hiro.

"The robots wrestle each other," said Toshiki. "The matches are like real sumo wrestling. Each robot tries to push the other robot out of

20   the ring."

Toshiki and Hiro watched Power Robot fight its first match. It was a good match. The two robots ran into each other again and again.

At last the match was over. Power Robot won! It pushed the other robot out of the ring.

25 Power Robot won the next three matches, too. Then it wrestled a robot named Tokyo Toy. This robot was too strong. It pushed Power Robot out of the circle, so Tokyo Toy won the tournament.

Toshiki was not sad. "Just wait until next year," he told Hiro. "I plan to return with Power Robot II."

Comprehension

True or False? Fill in the correct bubble.

1. Toshiki made Power Robot. . . . .(T) . . . . . . (F)

2. Toshiki won the tournament. . . . .(T) . . . . . . (F)

3. The tournament was in Kyoto, Japan. . . . .(T) . . . . . . (F)

4. Power Robot won five matches. . . . .(T) . . . . . . (F)

5. Toshiki thinks he can win next year. . . . .(T) . . . . . . (F)

Main Idea

What is the main idea of this story? Fill in the correct bubble.

(1) Robot sumo wrestling is popular in Japan.

(2) Toshiki doesn't win the tournament.

(3) Toshiki enters his robot in a big tournament.

(4) Robot sumo wrestling has the same rules as sumo wrestling.

Reading Skill: Understanding the Topic

Understanding the topic helps you know what the story is about. The **topic** is the subject or general idea. For example, the topic **famous cities** includes **Tokyo**, **Los Angeles**, and **London**.

Read each line. Underline the topic.

1. centimeter	<u>measurement</u>	kilograms	pounds
2. match	tournament	game	rules
3. computer	screen	keyboard	mouse
4. battery	robot parts	remote control	computer chips
5. Tokyo Toy	Power Robot	robot names	Power Robot II

Vocabulary Review

Complete the sentences. Fill in the correct bubble.

1. Power Robot only moves when Toshiki uses the _____.
   A screen   **B** remote control   **C** computer

2. Toshiki looks at a Web site on his computer _____.
   A screen   **B** robot   **C** printer

3. A _____ gives power to a machine.
   A kilogram   **B** battery   **C** computer

4. Toshiki turns on his _____ every day after school.
   A robot   **B** battery   **C** computer

5. A _____ is a machine that does something like a person.
   A tournament   **B** robot   **C** screen

Vocabulary Expansion: Learning Computer Terms

Today most people use computers. It is important to know common computer words.

1. Study the following terms.

   ■ The **desktop** is the screen you see when you start up a computer.
   ■ **Icons** are pictures or signs for computer programs.
   ■ A **menu** is a list of choices.
   ■ **Folders** have your personal files.

2. What is the name for each item on the computer screen? Write the correct word on the line.

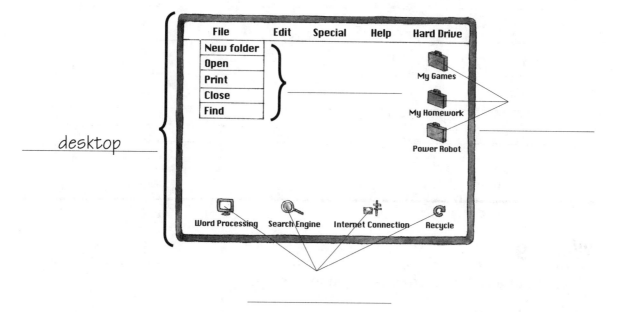

3. Add five new words from Chapter 14 to your Vocabulary Notebook on page 103.

Group Work: Comparing Free Time Activities

1. Work with a partner. Write five free time activities you like to do in the circle on the left.
   For example: I like robot wrestling, chess, mountain biking, basketball, and reading comic books.

2. Ask your partner about the free time activities he or she likes to do. Write his or her answers in the circle on the right.

3. Write activities you both like to do in the middle.

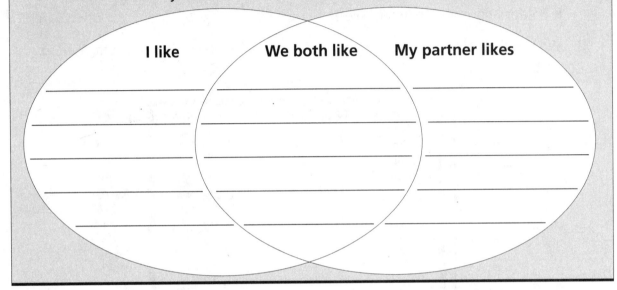

I like   **We both like**   **My partner likes**

Writing

Write about a club you are interested in joining.

1. I want to join a _____ club.

2. In this club people _____ .

3. I want to join this club because _____ .

Using the Internet

Do an Internet search about robot wrestling. Use a search engine like Yahoo!. Visit two Web sites or more. Tell a partner three new things you learned about robots.

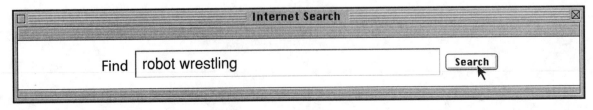

Internet Search

Find | robot wrestling | **Search**

CHAPTER 15

Saved by Dolphins

1. ocean   2. boat   3. dolphins   4. shark   5. swimmer

Key Vocabulary

Complete the sentences a word from the picture.

a. The _____ is a large and dangerous fish.

b. The men are watching _____ play in the water.

c. Sharks and dolphins swim in the _____.

d. The men in the _____ are wearing lifejackets.

e. The _____ in the water doesn't see the shark.

Before You Read

Look at the chapter title and the picture. Where are the men? Read the story to check your guess.

(A) At the ocean   (B) On a lake   (C) In a swimming pool

Saved by Dolphins

"Look over there!" said Robert.

Robert was on his **boat** with his friends, Bill and Tom Cooper. Five (dolphins) were near the boat. Robert was excited. He loved dolphins because they are friendly to people.

5   Robert moved to the side of the boat. For the next 30 minutes, he and his friends watched the dolphins jump and play in the (ocean.) At last the dolphins swam away. Robert could not see them anymore.

"I'm hot," said Robert. "Let's go for a swim."

"You go ahead," said Bill. "I'm not a very good (swimmer.) I think I'll

10 stay on the boat with Tom."

Robert jumped into the water. Bill and Tom sat in the warm sun as Robert swam away.

Suddenly Bill and Tom heard Robert scream. They ran to the side of the boat. They saw something in the water near Robert.

15 "It's a **shark**!" yelled Bill. "I see it! The shark is swimming right toward Robert!"

The two men did not know what to do. Then they saw something amazing. The five dolphins came back. The dolphins swam in a circle around Robert. They jumped into the air. They hit the water with their

20 tails. They kept the shark away from Robert.

"Look!" said Tom. "The shark is swimming away!"

Tom started the boat. He brought the boat over to Robert. The dolphins were still there, but the shark was gone. Bill and Tom pulled Robert into the boat. Robert was scared and shaking.

25   Tom put a towel around Robert's shoulders.

"Wow," said Bill. "That shark came really close to you."

"I know," said Robert, "but the dolphins saved me."

"Look! They're still here," said Tom. "They are right next to the boat."

Tom steered the boat back toward the beach. The dolphins followed

30 the boat. The dolphins did not leave until the boat reached the beach.

Then they turned and swam away.

Robert smiled when he saw them go. "Goodbye!" he shouted to

them. "And thank you!"

Comprehension

Complete the sentences. Fill in the correct bubble.

1. The dolphins _____ Robert.
   (A) helped   (B) hurt   (C) disliked

2. Bill didn't know how to _____ well.
   (A) scream   (B) talk   (C) swim

3. The dolphins hit the water with their _____.
   (A) tails   (B) heads   (C) noses

4. The dolphins followed the men back to the _____.
   (A) boat   (B) beach   (C) shark

5. Bill and Tom were _____ the shark.
   (A) happy about   (B) eaten by   (C) scared of

Main Idea

What is the main idea of this story? Fill in the correct bubble.

(1) Sharks don't like dolphins.

(2) Some dolphins save Robert from a shark.

(3) You should never go swimming alone.

(4) A shark saves Robert from some dolphins.

Reading Skill: Making Inferences

Making inferences helps you understand more about the story. To make an inference, you use what is said in a story to guess at something unsaid.

Information from the story
Tom and Bill heard a scream.

→

Inference
Robert was in danger.

Fill in the correct bubble to complete the sentences.

1. **Information:** Robert jumped into the ocean.
   Inference: He _____.
      (A) was in danger   (B) was a good swimmer

2. **Information:** Robert started to scream.
   Inference: Robert saw _____.
      (A) a shark   (B) dolphins

3. **Information:** The dolphins jumped into the air. They hit the water with their tails. They kept the shark away from Robert.
   Inference: The shark was _____.
      (A) tired   (B) scared

4. **Information:** The dolphins did not leave the boat until it reached the beach. Then they swam away.
   Inference: The dolphins wanted the men to be _____.
      (A) dry   (B) safe

Vocabulary Review

Complete the sentences. Write the missing word.

boat	dolphins	ocean	shark	swimmer

1. Robert likes to swim in the _____.

2. On Saturday he takes his _____ on the sea.

3. Sometimes he sees _____ swimming and playing in the water.

4. Robert is a good _____, but he always wears a lifejacket when he is on his boat.

5. People should never swim when there's a _____ in the water.

Vocabulary Expansion: Grouping Words

Grouping words can help you remember them. For example, **motorboats**, **sailboats**, and **ships** are words for different kinds of **boats**.

1. Cross out the word that does not belong in the group.

Group name: _Boats_

> motorboats
>
> sailboats
>
> ships
>
> ~~swimmers~~

Group name: _____

> boats
>
> helmets
>
> knee pads
>
> lifejackets

Group name: _____

> beach
>
> city
>
> sea
>
> water

Group name: _____

> dogs
>
> dolphins
>
> fish
>
> sharks

2. Write the group name above the correct box.

The ocean
Animals that live in water

~~Boats~~
Clothes that keep you safe

 3. Add five new words from Chapter 15 to your Vocabulary Notebook on page 104.

Group Work: Interviewing People About Helpful Animals

Interview five people. Ask them to name animals that help people. Ask them how the animals help people. Complete the chart.

Example:

A: What is an animal that helps people?
B: A dolphin helps people.
A: How does it help people?
B: It chases sharks away from swimmers.

Name	An animal that helps people	How the animal helps people
Robert	dolphin	chases sharks away from swimmers

Writing

Write about an animal that scares you.

1. An animal that scares me is _____.

2. This animal scares me because _____.

3. When I see this animal, I _____.

 ## Using the Internet

Do an Internet search about dolphins. Use a search engine like Yahoo!. Visit two Web sites or more. Tell a partner three things you learned about dolphins.

Internet Search	⊠

Find dolphins   [Search]

CHAPTER 16

An Underground Town

Key Vocabulary

Match the sentence and the picture. Write the number on the line.

a. One woman is looking at a **sign** for Coober Pedy. _____

b. The women drove on a **highway** to get to Coober Pedy. _____

c. Some buildings in the town are **underground**. They are not above ground. _____

d. The women can rent a room at the **motel**. _____

e. They can go to the **museum** to learn about history or art. _____

Before You Read

Look at the chapter title and the picture. What are the women doing? Read the story to check your guess.

(A) Going home   (B) Looking for a town   (C) Exercising

An Underground Town

See Page 116

Rita and Clara are old friends from California. Every year they go on a trip during their winter vacation. They like to travel to new places and see new things.

Last winter vacation Rita and Clara were in Australia for the first
5 time. They drove along the Stuart **Highway**. It went through a hot desert. Rita looked out the window. She saw nothing but sand. "Are you sure there is a town near here?" she asked.

"I think so," said Clara. "The map shows a place called Coober Pedy. It is just a few miles from here."

10 "Good," said Rita. "I'm tired of camping. I want to sleep in a **motel**. I don't want to sleep on the ground again."

They drove for another 10 minutes. Then Clara said, "Okay, this is Coober Pedy."

She and Rita looked around. Coober Pedy did not look like a big town.
15 Rita and Clara saw some homes. They also saw large pipes coming out of the ground.

"This town doesn't look very interesting," said Rita. She sighed. "Let's go on."

"Wait," said Clara. "Look over there. There is a **sign**. It says The
20 **Underground** Motel."

"What do you think that means?" asked Rita.

"I think it means there is a motel under that hill," Clara told her.

"You're kidding!" said Rita.

But Clara was right. The Underground Motel was underground. In

25 fact, many buildings in Coober Pedy are underground.

   Coober Pedy has many caves. A cave is a large underground hole. The air down in the caves is cool. People in Coober Pedy didn't like the hot desert sun. They started to build their homes inside the caves. They made one cave into a library. They made another cave into a **museum**. They also
30 built restaurants and churches underground. They put pipes down in the caves. The pipes bring in fresh air.

   Rita and Clara rented a room at The Underground Motel. They planned to stay one night, but Coober Pedy was so interesting that they stayed three days.

Comprehension

Complete the sentences. Fill in the correct bubble.

1. This was Rita and Clara's first trip _____.
   - (A) together
   - (B) to Australia
   - (C) to a new place

2. Rita didn't want to sleep on the _____.
   - (A) bed
   - (B) car
   - (C) ground

3. Some people in Coober Pedy live in _____.
   - (A) tents
   - (B) motels
   - (C) caves

4. Rita and Clara stayed in Coober Pedy for _____.
   - (A) three miles
   - (B) three hours
   - (C) three days

5. The women slept on the ground _____ they went to Coober Pedy.
   - (A) before
   - (B) three weeks after
   - (C) one night after

Main Idea

What is the main idea of this story? Fill in the correct bubble.

1. Two women find a strange and interesting town.

2. In Coober Pedy people live in caves.

3. Two women should not travel alone.

4. People in the desert live in different kinds of homes.

Reading Skill: Putting Events in Order

> **Putting events in order** helps you understand the story's action. To put events in order, look for words that say when an event happened. For example, look for **first**, **second**, **next**, and **last**.

Fill in the sentences with the correct word from the box.

~~First~~	Second	Next	Last

1. _____, they arrived in the next town.

2. _____First_____, Rita and Clara stayed in Coober Pedy for three days.

3. _____, Rita looked on the map for a new town to visit.

4. _____, Rita and Clara checked into a motel in the new town.

Vocabulary Review

Complete the sentences. Fill in the correct bubble.

1. People stay at a **motel** when they are _____.
   - Ⓐ on a trip
   - Ⓑ at home
   - Ⓒ camping

2. In Coober Pedy, people live **underground** in _____.
   - Ⓐ museums
   - Ⓑ tents
   - Ⓒ caves

3. On the **highway**, a lot of _____ go very fast.
   - Ⓐ paintings
   - Ⓑ cars
   - Ⓒ maps

4. When people are lost, they look for a **sign** to give them _____.
   - Ⓐ fresh air
   - Ⓑ information
   - Ⓒ a tent

5. At the **museum** people can see _____ or learn about history.
   - Ⓐ trucks
   - Ⓑ money
   - Ⓒ art

Vocabulary Expansion: Grouping Words

Putting words into groups can help you remember them.
For example, **schools, colleges,** and **universities** are **places to study.**

1. Look at the pictures.

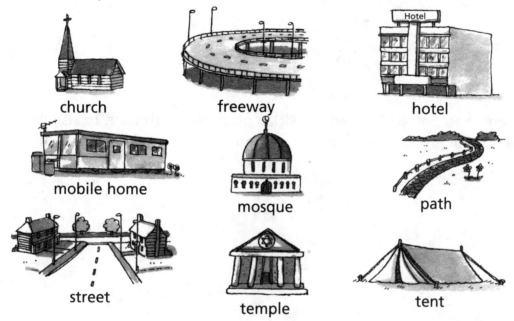

church   freeway   hotel

mobile home

mosque   path

street   temple   tent

2. Write the words in the correct boxes.

Roads	Places to sleep	Religious Buildings

3. Add five new words from Chapter 16 to your Vocabulary Notebook on page 104.

Group Work: Planning a Vacation

1. Look at Rita and Clara's to-do list.

✔ get plane tickets
✔ get maps
✔ reserve a car at airport
✔ pack the tent
✔ buy a guidebook

2. Plan a vacation with a partner. Pick a place you both want to visit. Write eight things you must do before you go.

Planning list for a trip to _____
1. _____
2. _____
3. _____
4. _____
5. _____
6. _____
7. _____
8. _____

3. Find another pair of students. Tell them about your plans.

Writing

Write about your favorite vacation.

1. On my favorite vacation I went to _____.

2. I went with _____.

3. The best thing about my vacation was _____.

Using the Internet

Do an Internet search about Australia. Use a search engine like Yahoo!. Visit two Web sites or more. Tell a partner three new things you learned about Australia.

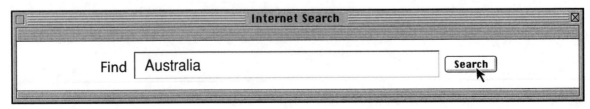

Internet Search

Find | Australia | Search

Vocabulary Notebook

Chapter 1   Driving a Taxi in New York

Word	Sample Sentence
passenger	The passenger is in the taxi.
1. _____	_____
2. _____	_____
3. _____	_____
4. _____	_____
5. _____	_____

Chapter 2   Running the Boston Marathon

Word	Sample Sentence
noon	I eat lunch at noon.
1. _____	_____
2. _____	_____
3. _____	_____
4. _____	_____
5. _____	_____

Vocabulary Notebook

Chapter 3   The Search for Bobby

Word	Sample Sentence
ground	The woman walks on the ground.
1.	
2.	
3.	
4.	
5.	

Chapter 4   Kindness in the Desert

Word	Sample Sentence
thirsty	The thirsty boy wants some water.
1.	
2.	
3.	
4.	
5.	

Vocabulary Notebook

Chapter 5   Don't Throw That Food Away

Word	Sample Sentence
bakery	You buy bread and cake at a bakery.
1. _____	_____
2. _____	_____
3. _____	_____
4. _____	_____
5. _____	_____

Chapter 6   A Home Full of Children

Word	Sample Sentence
closet	I keep my clothes in the closet.
1. _____	_____
2. _____	_____
3. _____	_____
4. _____	_____
5. _____	_____

Vocabulary Notebook

Chapter 7 — Biking Down a Volcano

Word	Sample Sentence
beach	I like to swim at the beach.
1.	
2.	
3.	
4.	
5.	

Chapter 8 — The Flood

Word	Sample Sentence
scared	My brother is scared of spiders.
1.	
2.	
3.	
4.	
5.	

Vocabulary Notebook

Chapter 9   First Day of School

Word	Sample Sentence
cafeteria	My friends eat lunch in the cafeteria.
1.	
2.	
3.	
4.	
5.	

Chapter 10   Grandmother's Bear Paw Soup

Word	Sample Sentence
spices	Salt and pepper are spices.
1.	
2.	
3.	
4.	
5.	

Vocabulary Notebook

Chapter 11   Golfing in a Storm

Word	Sample Sentence
wind	The wind blew my paper out of my hand.
1. _____	_____
2. _____	_____
3. _____	_____
4. _____	_____
5. _____	_____
_____	_____

Chapter 12   Lost on a Mountain

Word	Sample Sentence
gloves	Gloves make your hands warm.
1. _____	_____
2. _____	_____
3. _____	_____
4. _____	_____
5. _____	_____
_____	_____

Vocabulary Notebook

Chapter 13   A Cat Saves a Family

Word	Sample Sentence
kitchen	She cooks dinner in the kitchen.
1.	
2.	
3.	
4.	
5.	

Chapter 14   Robot Wrestling

Word	Sample Sentence
battery	My cell phone needs a battery.
1.	
2.	
3.	
4.	
5.	

Vocabulary Notebook

Chapter 15   Saved by Dolphins

Word	Sample Sentence
shark	It's dangerous to swim with a shark.
1. _____	_____
2. _____	_____
3. _____	_____
4. _____	_____
5. _____	_____

Chapter 16   An Underground Town

Word	Sample Sentence
highway	People drive fast on the highway.
1. _____	_____
2. _____	_____
3. _____	_____
4. _____	_____
5. _____	_____

Vocabulary Notebook

Word

Sample Sentence

Vocabulary Notebook

Word

Sample Sentence

——————————— ————————————————————————

——————————— ————————————————————————

——————————— ————————————————————————

——————————— ————————————————————————

——————————— ————————————————————————

——————————— ————————————————————————

——————————— ————————————————————————

——————————— ————————————————————————

——————————— ————————————————————————

——————————— ————————————————————————

Irregular Verb Chart

Present Tense	Past Tense	Past Participle
am / is / are	was, were	been
begin	began	begun
blow	blew	blown
break	broke	broken
bring	brought	brought
build	built	built
burn	burned	burned
buy	bought	bought
come	came	come
cost	cost	cost
cut	cut	cut
do	did	done
drink	drank	drunk
drive	drove	driven
eat	ate	eaten
fall	fell	fallen
feel	felt	felt
find	found	found
fly	flew	flown
forget	forgot	forgotten
get	got	gotten, got
give	gave	given
go	went	gone
grow	grew	grown
have	had	had
hear	heard	heard
know	knew	known
learn	learned	learned

Present Tense	Past Tense	Past Participle
leave	left	left
lose	lost	lost
make	made	made
meet	met	met
pay	paid	paid
put	put	put
read	read	read
ride	rode	ridden
run	ran	run
say	said	said
see	saw	seen
sell	sold	sold
send	sent	sent
sing	sang	sung
sit	sat	sat
sleep	slept	slept
speak	spoke	spoken
spend	spent	spent
stand	stood	stood
swim	swam	swum
take	took	taken
teach	taught	taught
tell	told	told
think	thought	thought
throw	threw	thrown
understand	understood	understood
wear	wore	worn
win	won	won
write	wrote	written

Skills Index

READING

Comprehension
factual: 3, 9, 15, 21, 27, 33, 39, 45, 51, 57, 63, 69, 75, 81, 87, 93
inferential: 3, 9, 15, 21, 27, 33, 39, 45, 51, 57, 63, 69, 75, 81, 87, 93
main idea: 3, 9, 15, 21, 27, 33, 39, 45, 51, 57, 63, 69, 75, 81, 87, 93

Skills
finding details: 10, 28, 64
identifying cause and effect: 4, 58, 76
sequencing: 16, 52, 70, 94
making inferences: 22, 40, 88
understanding topic of a selection: 34, 46, 82

Literary Content
adoption: 32–33
animals: 14–15, 74–75
blindness: 8
charity: 20–21, 74–75
family life: 32–33, 74–75
firefighting: 74–75
food and drink: 56–57
geography: 20–21, 38–39, 44–45, 56–57, 86–87, 92–93
home layouts: 32–33, 74–75
occupations: 2, 14–15, 26–27, 56–57
police and rangers: 14–15, 68–69
rescue: 14–15, 68–69, 74–75, 86–87
sports: 8, 38–39, 86–87
technology: 80–81
weather: 44–45, 61–67

Pre-Reading Questions
1, 7, 13, 19, 25, 31, 37, 43, 49, 55, 57, 61, 67, 73, 79, 85, 91

Critical Thinking
1, 7, 13, 19, 25, 31, 37, 43, 49, 55, 61, 67, 73, 79, 85, 91

Reading Through Art
1, 7, 13, 19, 25, 31, 37, 43, 49, 55, 61, 67, 73, 79, 85, 91

WRITING
answers to questions about your town: 72
club you would like to join: 84
description of your bedroom: 78
description of your family: 36
enjoyable outdoor activity: 42
enjoyable sport to watch: 12
favorite city: 66
favorite foods: 24, 60
favorite season: 6
favorite teacher: 54
favorite vacation: 96
home city: 48
scary animal: 90
seeing, hearing, smelling: 18
something you buy every week: 30

VOCABULARY
introduction of: 1, 7, 13, 19, 25, 31, 37, 43, 49, 55, 61, 67, 73, 79, 85, 91
in context: 4, 10, 16, 22, 28, 40, 46, 52, 58, 64, 70, 76, 82, 88, 94
expansion of: 5, 11, 17, 23, 29, 35, 41, 47, 53, 59, 65, 71, 77, 83, 89, 95
grouping of words: 5, 11, 17, 23, 29, 35, 41, 47, 53, 59, 65, 71, 77, 83, 89, 95
opposite pairs: 47
question words: 28
word forms: 65

Vocabulary Index

Chapter 5

bakery
bank
block
bread
buy
car
clothing shop
doctor
fill up
gas station
health clinic
homeless shelter
letter
neighborhood
money
post office
send
supermarket
sweater
withdraw

Chapter 6

bedroom
clothes
closet
cook
dining room
dress
eat
hang up
kitchen
living room
read
relax
sleep
study

Chapter 7

bait
baseball
beach

fishing
fishing pole
forest
glove
golf
helmet
hiking
hook
lake
mountain biking
net
pump
running
sailing
skiing
soccer
swimming
tennis
volleyball
waders
water bottle

Chapter 8

bad
brave
city
country
dangerous
flood
good
leave
old
rain
river
safe
scared
stay
sunshine
young

Chapter 9

blackboard
cafeteria
chairs
classroom
computer lab
desk
English
gym
library
locker
main office
principal
science lab

Chapter 10

apples
bananas
chef
dairy products
fats
fruit
grains
milk
mushrooms
oils
oranges
protein
recipe
rice
soup
spices
sweets
vegetables

Chapter 11

cloud
fog
foggy
lightning
rain
rainy
snow
snowy

storm
sun
sunny
thunder
wind
windy

Chapter 12

backpack
boots
coat
gloves
hat
jacket
mittens
pants
pair
raincoat
shirt
shoes
sneakers
socks
sweater
whistle

Chapter 13

backyard
bed
bedroom
curtains
dresser
grill
kitchen
lamp
pan
picnic table
plates
pot
refrigerator
sink
stairs
stove
swing set

Chapter 14

battery
computer
desktop
folder
icon
menu
remote control
robot
screen

Chapter 15

boat
city
dog
dolphin
fish
helmet
knee pad
lifejacket
motorboat
ocean
sailboat
sea
shark
ship
swimmer
water

Chapter 16

cave
church
freeway
hotel
highway
mobile home
mosque
motel
museum
path
sign
street
temple
tent
underground

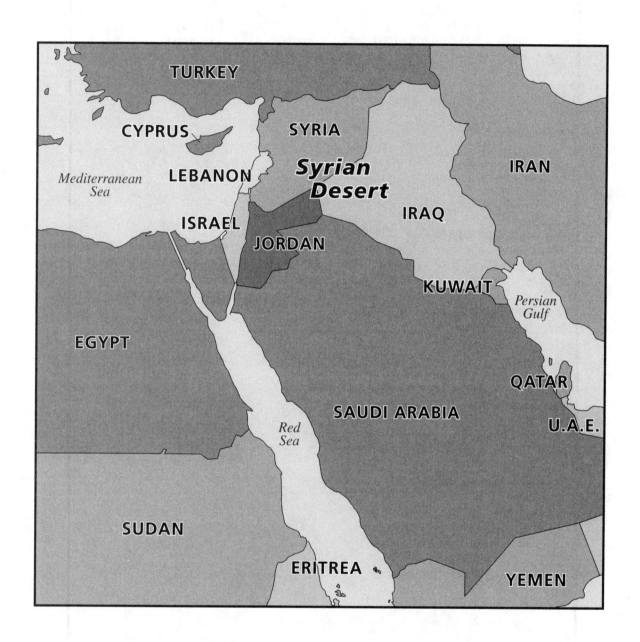

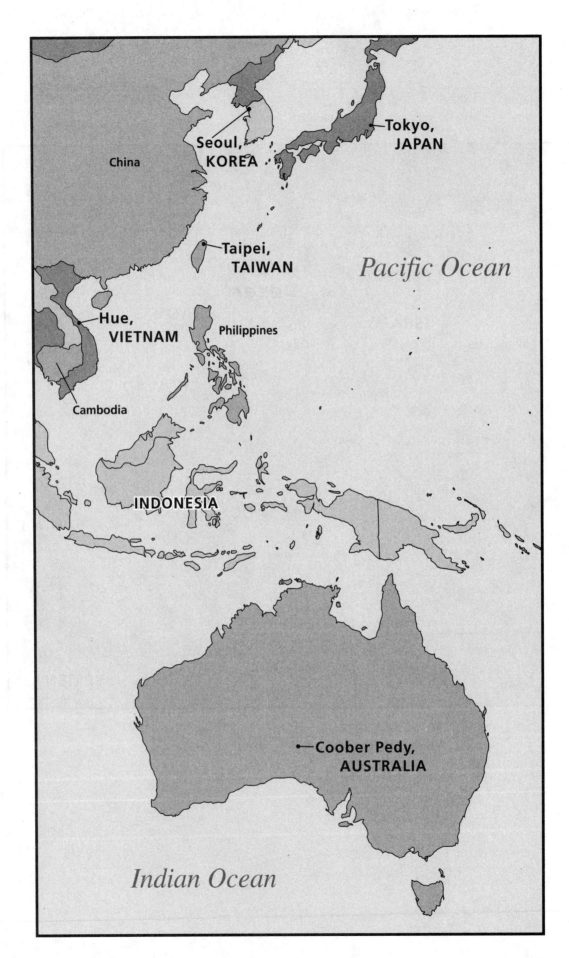

China

Seoul,
KOREA

Tokyo,
JAPAN

Taipei,
TAIWAN

Pacific Ocean

Hue,
VIETNAM

Philippines

Cambodia

INDONESIA

Coober Pedy,
AUSTRALIA

Indian Ocean